AQA History

Twentieth Century Depth Studies

GCSE

David Ferriby

Tony Hewitt

Jim McCabe

Alan Mendum

Nelson Thornes

Published in 2009 by:
Nelson Thornes Ltd
Delta Place
27 Bath Road
CHELTENHAM
GL53 7TH
United Kingdom

09 10 11 12 13 / 10 9 8 7 6 5 4 3 2 1

A catalogue record for this book is available from the British Library

ISBN 978 1 4085 0321 8

Cover photograph by Topfoto/John Mitchell
Illustrations by David Russell Illustration, Fakenham Photosetting Ltd
Page make-up by Fakenham Photosetting Ltd

Printed and bound in Spain by GraphyCems

Contents

Nelson Thornes and AQA   4

Introduction   5

SECTION A

1 From Tsardom to Communism: Russia, 1914–24   6

1.1 Why did the rule of the Tsar collapse in February/March 1917?   6

1.2 Why were the Bolsheviks able to seize power in October/November 1917?   16

1.3 How successful was Lenin in creating a new society in Russia?   22

2 Weimar Germany, 1919–29   34

2.1 How far do the early problems of the Weimar Republic suggest that it was doomed from the start?   34

2.2 How far did the Weimar Republic recover under Stresemann?   44

2.3 How far did the Nazi Party develop its ideas and organisation up to 1929?   48

3 The Roaring 20s: USA, 1919–29   54

3.1 How and why did the USA achieve prosperity in the 1920s?   54

3.2 How far was the USA a divided society in the 1920s?   63

3.3 Why did the US Stock Exchange collapse in 1929?   72

SECTION B

4 Stalin's dictatorship: USSR, 1924–41   76

4.1 To what extent had Stalin become a personal dictator in communist Russia by the end of the 1920s?   76

4.2 How did Stalin reinforce his dictatorship, 1929–41?   82

4.3 To what extent did Stalin make the USSR a great economic power?   88

5 Hitler's Germany, 1929–39   94

5.1 How and why was Hitler able to become Chancellor in January 1933?   94

5.2 How did Hitler change Germany from a democracy to a Nazi dictatorship, 1933–34?   98

5.3 To what extent did Germans benefit from Nazi rule in the 1930s?   109

6 Depression and the New Deal: the USA, 1929–41   118

6.1 How serious were the effects of the Depression on the American people?   118

6.2 How did Roosevelt deal with the Depression?   125

6.3 How far was the New Deal successful in ending the Depression in the USA?   131

7 Race relations in the USA, 1955–68   136

7.1 To what extent did racial inequality exist in the USA in the 1950s?   136

7.2 How effective were the methods used by members of the Civil Rights movement between 1961 and 1968?   144

7.3 How important was Martin Luther King in the fight for civil rights in the USA?   152

8 The USA and Vietnam: failure abroad and at home, 1964–75   160

8.1 How effective were the guerrilla tactics during the Vietnam War?   160

8.2 How did the coverage of the Vietnam War in the USA lead to demands for peace?   170

8.3 Why were the US actions to end the Vietnam War unsuccessful?   175

9 Britain: the challenge in Northern Ireland, 1960–86   184

9.1 How far did political and economic inequalities lead to the Troubles in the 1960s and 1970s?   184

9.2 Why was it difficult to find a solution to the Troubles in the 1960s and 1970s?   191

9.3 How far from peace was Ireland by the mid-1980s?   200

10 The Middle East, 1956–79   210

10.1 How far did the years 1956–67 show how difficult it was to find a solution to the problems in the Middle East?   210

10.2 How close to victory were the Arabs in the 1970s?   220

10.3 How close to peace was the Middle East by the end of the 1970s?   226

Glossary   233

Index   235

Nelson Thornes and AQA

Nelson Thornes has worked in partnership with AQA to ensure this book and the accompanying online resources offer you the best support for your GCSE course.

All resources have been approved by senior AQA examiners so you can feel assured that they closely match the specification for this subject and provide you with everything you need to prepare successfully for your exams.

These print and online resources together **unlock blended learning**; this means that the links between the activities in the book and the activities online blend together to maximise your understanding of a topic and help you achieve your potential.

These online resources are available on *kerboodle!* which can be accessed via the internet at **www.kerboodle.com/live**, anytime, anywhere. If your school or college subscribes to *kerboodle!* you will be provided with your own personal login details. Once logged in, access your course and locate the required activity.

For more information and help on how to use *kerboodle!* visit **www.kerboodle.com**.

How to use this book

Objectives

Look for the list of **Learning Objectives** based on the requirements of this course so you can ensure you are covering everything you need to know for the exam.

AQA Examiner's tip

Don't forget to read the **AQA Examiner's Tips** throughout the book as well as practice answering **Examination-style Questions**.

Visit **www.nelsonthornes.com/aqagcse** for more information.

AQA examination-style questions are reproduced by permission of the Assessment and Qualifications Alliance.

■ Unit 2: 20th Century Depth Studies

This book covers all the material required for the study of *AQA GCSE History Specification B Unit 2: 20th Century Depth Studies*. It focuses on particular countries and small periods of time to allow a more detailed study of events and personalities. Whilst some depth studies are centred on the period between the two World Wars, others focus on more recent history. It is intended that the depth studies on this Unit will be seen as complementary to the international outlines studied for Unit 1.

You will notice that this book has 10 chapters, each one corresponding to one of the depth studies of Unit 2 of the specification. The title of each chapter is the same as the heading given for each depth study. Within each depth study in the specification there are three key issues, and within each key issue there are bullet points that indicate the historical knowledge needed. Similarly, each chapter of the book has three subtitles that are the key issues highlighted in the specification as the focus for study. The sub-headings and text that follow cover all the bullet points in the specification.

In the GCSE examination for Unit 2, there will be 10 questions set, one on each of the 10 chapters in the book. However, the questions in the examination are divided into two sections. Section A covers Chapters 1–3, and in the examination you have to answer the question on one of these chapters. Section B covers Chapters 4–10, and you have to answer questions on two of these chapters. Therefore, your school will have decided which chapters you will be concentrating on. If you have covered these chapters thoroughly, you will be certain that you have enough historical information and understanding to answer three questions in the examination.

The types of examination question are different for Sections A and B. In each question in Section A there will be a comprehension-type question – a question requiring explanation of an event or situation – and a question testing the utility of a source. In Section B, each question has two parts: a description question and an analytical essay.

This book guides you through the history of the period and also has a series of tasks and activities that are designed to help you check your understanding of the issues and give you practice in evaluating a variety of sources. Many of these tasks contain questions similar to those that you will see in the GCSE examination. At the end of each chapter, you are given an example of an examination-style question that shows you the mark allocation for each part of the question.

1 From Tsardom to Communism: Russia, 1914–24

1.1 Why did the rule of the Tsar collapse in February/March 1917?

A *Tsar Nicholas II*

Objectives

In this chapter you will learn about:

the causes of the first revolution following the Tsar's abdication in February/March 1917

why the Bolsheviks were able to seize power in October/November 1917 in a second revolution

how successful Lenin was in creating a new communist society.

In early 1914, the Russian Empire, vast and backward, had been ruled by the Romanov tsars for 300 years. On the surface, nothing appeared to be changing. However, in 1917, two revolutions happened – the **Tsar** was forced to give up his throne and seven months later the revolutionary Bolshevik Party seized control. Their leader, Lenin, then tried hard in the next few years to create a new society – the first communist country in the world.

The government of Nicholas II in 1914

Russia was an **autocracy**. Its ruler, Tsar Nicholas II, had been on the throne for 20 years. He believed that he ruled Russia on behalf of God, and therefore no one had the right to challenge him. His family, the Romanovs, had ruled Russia for 300 years.

His wife, Alexandra, had been a German princess. They had four daughters, all greatly loved, but Nicholas and Alexandra were desperate to have a son who would succeed to the throne. When a boy, whom they named Alexis, was born, there was great rejoicing throughout the empire. However, it was soon discovered that the boy had haemophilia, a blood disease that meant his blood would not clot. If he cut himself, he could bleed to death. Far worse was internal bleeding following any knock or bump. He was protected as much as possible from injuries as he grew up. Only a small number of people knew what was actually wrong with whom they assumed was a rather sickly boy.

Key terms

Tsar: the Russian version of Emperor.

Autocracy: rule by someone who has complete power.

Russian Orthodox Church: the Christian Church in Russia.

Duma: a representative assembly, or parliament, first set up in 1905 as a concession by the Tsar. However, the Tsar made sure that the Duma had little power.

Okhrana: secret police force of the Russian Empire.

In theory, the Tsar was all-powerful. Priests in the **Russian Orthodox Church** supported this claim. The Tsar had advisers, whom he appointed, but he made the decisions. Unfortunately, he was not very good at this.

The Tsar had been forced in 1905 to allow a *Duma* to be elected, but it had little power and was heavily dominated by the educated upper and middle classes. The Tsar could dismiss it whenever he wished and he was not forced to take any notice of what it wanted.

The actual government was cumbersome, inefficient and slow. Hampered by poor communications, information took months to be received. However, the Tsar's wishes were enforced by the secret police, the *Okhrana*. Newspapers and books were censored.

B *Alexis and Nicholas II in military uniform*

Timeline

Key events in Russian history, 1914–24

1914	Tsar Nicholas II ruled vast Russian Empire.
1915	Tsar made himself Commander-in-Chief of Russian armies.
1916	Death of Rasputin.
1917 Feb/ Mar	Tsar abdicated; Provisional Government took over.
1917 Oct/ Nov	Bolsheviks under Lenin seized control.
1918 Mar	Treaty of Brest-Litovsk.
	Start of Russian Civil War.
1918 Jul	Execution of Romanov royal family.
	Policy of War Communism started.
1921	End of Russian Civil War.
	Start of the NEP.
1922 Dec	Declaration of USSR.
1923	Lenin seriously ill following stroke.
1924 Jan	Death of Lenin.

Did you know ??????

The marriage of Nicholas and Alexandra was arranged for them. At first, they agreed out of a sense of duty. Later, they fell in love. However, his main language was Russian, hers was German. They spoke to each other mostly in English.

The nature of Russian society in 1914

Tsar Nicholas II ruled not just a country, but a huge empire. It spread across the continents of Europe and Asia and stretched across eight time zones. Its population was over 125 million, but only 55 million were Russian. As the empire had expanded in previous centuries, many other nationalities had been included, such as Finns, Poles, Ukrainians, Estonians, Lithuanians and Georgians. They had their own languages and their own religions, such as Roman Catholic Christians in Poland and Muslims in the south of the empire near the Black Sea. In the north, people lived in the Arctic Circle; in the south, there were nomads living in tents in semi-desert areas.

C *Map of the Russian Empire*

Most of the people living in the Russian Empire were peasants, and there was a huge contrast between them and the rich nobles. The peasants had only recently had the right to possess their own land, but they had little machinery and were desperately poor. They farmed on strips of land with old-fashioned tools, as had happened for centuries. A poor harvest would mean famine and many deaths. The nobles, by contrast, were immensely rich, owning ornate palaces that rivalled those of the Tsar.

The process of industrialisation had started in Russia in thé 19th century, with industries such as coal mining, iron, steel and textiles. However, conditions in the rapidly expanding cities of Moscow and St Petersburg were even worse than those in the countryside.

The importance of traditional loyalties

In spite of the huge inequalities within the Russian Empire, most Russian peasants were intensely loyal to their country and to the Tsar. The peasants were religious (even though their beliefs were often mixed up with popular beliefs and superstitions). They obeyed their priests by being patriotic to Mother Russia and thought of the Tsar (whom most of them would never see) as their father-figure. The army was loyal to the Tsar. Although there were discontented elements within the empire, the structure of society gave the impression of stability and an ability to resist change.

66 *Never forget you are and must remain the autocratic Tsar. We are not yet ready for a democratic government. God anointed you at your coronation. He placed you where you stand. The people need to feel an iron will and hand. You are the Lord and Master in Russia. They shall bow down before your wisdom and firmness.* 99

E *From a letter to the Tsar from his wife, Alexandra, in 1915*

Tasks

1 Explain the difference between autocracy and democracy.

2 Using what you have read so far in this chapter, do you think that Russia was an easy country to rule in the early 20th century?

D *Contrasting images of rich and poor within Russian society*

The existence of opposition groups

There were, however, people who wanted change. Russia itself was changing with the process of industrialisation. Some Russians were becoming more educated and more aware of different methods of ruling a country. The Tsar did not allow political opposition and the Okhrana hunted down suspects. However, opposition groups had developed.

- The *Kadets* (Constitutional Democrats) were a middle-class liberal party that wanted peaceful political change with the elected Duma gaining real power – just as parliament had done in Victorian Britain. However, their support was mostly limited to more wealthy and more educated people living in towns and cities.

- The Social Revolutionaries (the SRs) wanted to seize power by revolution. They had some support from the peasants, as the plan was to take land from the landlords (the nobles) and give it to them. However, it was difficult to organise the peasants, scattered as they were across large areas of land.

- The Social Democrats had support mostly from workers in the factories. They believed in the communist teachings of Karl Marx. However, in 1903, the Social Democrats had split into two groups – the *Mensheviks* and the *Bolsheviks*. The Bolsheviks were the smaller group who believed that revolution was possible, even if they did not have mass support, if it was plotted in secret and carried out ruthlessly. The leader of the Bolsheviks was Lenin.

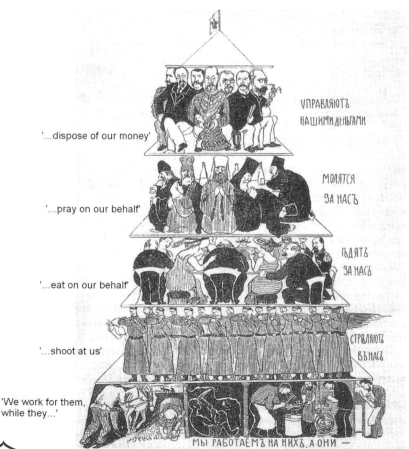

'...dispose of our money'

'...pray on our behalf'

'...eat on our behalf'

'...shoot at us'

'We work for them, while they...'

F *An artist's view of Russian society before 1914 using the idea of a tiered wedding cake*

Task

3   Study Source **F**. What is the artist trying to show about Russian society in the years before 1914?

■ The impact of the First World War on Russia

In August 1914, Russia declared war on Germany and on Austria-Hungary. Russia, therefore, was faced with fighting two huge Europe-based empires on what became known as the Eastern Front. On the Western Front, Germany was also fighting a range of allies headed by France and Britain.

Russia's army was huge (over 6 million men in 1914), but Russia lacked industry and had a system of government that was inefficient and corrupt. It was assumed that the war would be short. The Minister of War, Sukhomlinov, was told that 6.4 million men had to share 4.6 million rifles. Soldiers were told to limit themselves to 10 bullets a day. Military uniforms were also in short supply, with many soldiers not being properly equipped with winter uniforms. The army commanders were nobles, often with little relevant military experience.

To begin with, Russian military orders were not even sent in code and the Germans found it easy to intercept secret messages. This told them of the Russian positions and helped to explain why the Russians suffered military defeats. Trenches were often poorly built and provided little protection from the artillery fire of the enemy.

Initially, there was much patriotism; Russians were fighting to defend their homeland against the Germans and Austrians. Patriotism was often linked with religious fervour, with the priests playing an important role in ensuring support for the war.

Russia could sometimes win victories over Austria-Hungary, but could not achieve the same success against Germany. For example, in August and September 1914, Germany defeated Russia at the Battles of Tannenberg and Masurian Lakes. Russia suffered over a million casualties. After this, the German armies advanced deep into Russian territory.

In 1915, the Tsar decided to take over personal control as Commander-in-Chief of the armies. This was potentially disastrous as his indecisive character made him totally unsuitable. Any defeats would be seen as his personal responsibility, and it meant leaving Alexandra (a German princess!) in charge in the capital – now renamed Petrograd to make it less German-sounding.

In 1916, the Russians launched a major offensive against Austria led by General Brusilov. After initial advances, the Russian armies were forced to retreat, and another million Russians were killed or wounded. By the end of 1916, the Russian army was totally demoralised and near mutiny; some soldiers were deserting their posts.

Did you know ??????

The Russian army of the First World War is often referred to as 'The Russian Steamroller' due to the huge population of Tsarist Russia at the time. Recruits were mainly conscripted (usually illiterate) peasants.

Did you know ??????

The Russian capital of St Petersburg has also been called Petrograd and Leningrad. It ceased to be the capital city in 1918 after the Russian Revolution in 1917.

■ The effects of the war on the cities

The effects of the war were increasingly felt in the cities. There were food shortages, with prices rising by up to 700 per cent over three years. Workers' wages only increased by 200 per cent during the same period. Food was in short supply because much good farming land was occupied by the Germans. In some areas there was a shortage of peasants on the land as so many had been conscripted into the armies.

Also, transport was inefficiently organised. Engines and trucks would be commandeered for moving troops or supplies, leaving food for the cities rotting in railway sidings. Many railway engineers had been called up to fight, leaving a shortage of skilled people to carry out basic repairs to engines and trucks.

> ❝ Military defeats have brought the people of Russia closer to an understanding of war – unfair distribution of foodstuffs, an immense rise in the cost of living, and huge shortages. Everywhere there are exceptional feelings of hostility and opposition to the government because of the unbearable burden of the war and the impossible conditions of everyday life. ❞
>
> Taken from a secret police report in Petrograd, dated October 1916

G *The effects of war on the people of Petrograd*

I *Number of Russian railway engines in working order*

Year	Russian railway engines
1914	20,000
1917	9,000

J *Number of wagons of grain reaching Moscow per year*

Year	Wagons of grain
1913	22,000
1917	700

H *A Russian postcard issued in May 1916 showing the Tsar as Commander-in-Chief*

Tasks

4 What does Source **G** suggest about the effects of the war on the attitudes of the Russian peasants?

5 How useful is Source **H** for studying attitudes to the Tsar in his role of Commander-in-Chief? Use Source **H** and your own knowledge to explain your answer.

◼ The growing unpopularity of the Romanovs

When the war started, Romanov rule seemed secure. However, by 1916, the royal family was very unpopular. Part of this was due to the defeats and hardships, leading to the collapse of patriotism. But it was also due to the consequences of the Tsar going to the front. He left Alexandra in charge, with the Duma (parliament) to advise her. Alexandra was already unpopular due to her German background, but she was also very much under the influence of Rasputin, a peasant from Siberia who claimed to be a holy man. In fact, he was a womaniser and was believed (wrongly) to have been having an affair with Alexandra. His huge influence came from his alleged power over Alexis' haemophilia. When Alexis suffered internal bleeding, Rasputin appeared to be able to stop it. Rasputin had almost hypnotic powers over Alexandra, who was naturally desperate to keep him at court and refused to listen to any criticism of him. Meanwhile, Rasputin influenced the government by 'recommending' changes in ministers and getting his friends appointed to prominent positions.

Leading nobles (related to the royal family) detested Rasputin. In December 1916, a group of them, led by Prince Yusopov, killed him. But it was too late to save the monarchy. The government of the Russian Empire had reached crisis point.

Did you know ???????

Rasputin was often referred to as the 'Mad Monk'.

◼ *Rasputin at court*

Rasputin

The traditional story about the death of Rasputin says that he was lured to a private party by Prince Yusopov and some of his friends. Rasputin was given poisoned cakes and wine. When this did not kill him, Yusopov shot him with a pistol. Rasputin was still alive, so he was shoved through a hole in the ice of the River Neva. When Rasputin's corpse was found, it was discovered that he had died by drowning because water was found in his lungs.

However, historians have recently been able to investigate Russian archives, where police records tell a different story. According to these, he was shot by masked men who dumped his body in the River Neva. A post-mortem investigation found no poison in his bloodstream.

The traditional story was published by Yusopov, who admitted murder but escaped punishment. He lived until 1967, retaining hero status for ending the life of a super-human but evil mystic, even though Yusopov modified the details of his alleged exploits from time to time.

Did you know ???????

Prince Yusopov is well known for his part in the murder of Rasputin, but he also played an important role in aiding the poor. He was heir to a huge fortune and spent his time and his money on charitable works.

From 1909 to 1912, he studied at University College Oxford, where he established the Oxford University Russian Society.

Task

6 How useful is Source J for studying the effects of Rasputin on attitudes to the Russian monarchy?

Use Source J and your own knowledge to explain your answer.

J *A Russian cartoon showing Rasputin with the Tsar and Tsarina*

The revolution of March 1917: the abdication of the Tsar

The winter of 1916–17 was exceptionally severe – the coldest for a long time. In Petrograd, the temperature reached –35°C. Fuel froze. Women queued for hours to buy basic necessities such as bread.

In Petrograd, many people were starving to death. Strikes broke out and factory workers met in huge crowds in the streets. On 8 March (which was International Women's Day), 90,000 people were on strike in Petrograd, and there were demonstrations against the shortage of bread and fuel. Strikes spread, including the Putilov armaments works which employed 40,000 people.

On succeeding days, large numbers of people were in the streets with slogans such as 'Down with the German woman!' and 'Down with the Tsar!' Nicholas II ordered the army commander in Petrograd to crush the marchers and rioters. Increasingly, regiments refused to obey orders, and many of the officers fled. Petrograd was in the hands of the rioting mob.

In desperation, Rodzianko, President of the Duma, telegraphed the Tsar to inform him of the seriousness of the situation. The Tsar ignored the warning, preferring instead to read the telegraph from his wife telling him that the disturbances would soon be under control. The Duma reluctantly decided to take over the control of the government. At the same time, the workers organised themselves into a soviet (workers' council) in Petrograd.

The Tsar at last tried to return to Petrograd. He reached Pskov where the railway line was blocked. His train was moved into a siding and he was persuaded by Russian army commanders to abdicate. He tried to pass the throne to his brother Michael, but he refused. Alexis, of course, was not fit to rule. Therefore, over 300 years of Romanov history ended on 15 March 1917.

Did you know ???????

Russia used the old Julian Calendar, which was 13 days behind the Gregorian calendar used in Western Europe. Therefore, using the Russian calendar, the events of this first revolution happened in late February with the Tsar abdicating on 2 March.

In 1918, Lenin announced that Russia would use the same dates as the rest of Europe.

Did you know ???????

Rodzianko was not one of Rasputin's supporters. He believed that the ties between Rasputin and Tsar Nicholas II 'marked the beginning of the decay of the Russian society and the loss of prestige of the throne and of the Tsar himself'.

K *People queuing up for bread, February 1917*

Why were the Bolsheviks able to seize power in October/November 1917?

The problems facing the Provisional Government

The March 1917 revolution had not been planned. It was a spontaneous outpouring caused by despair and suffering that resulted from the war. No group had planned to take control; no group had planned what to do if there was no tsar because, to almost everyone, that thought was impossible.

Therefore, the Provisional Government (at first under Prince Lvov and from July 1917 under Alexander Kerensky) faced many daunting problems.

- The Provisional Government members were unused to making decisions. Their previous role had been limited to advising the Tsar. Now they had to make decisions, but these were questioned by the **Petrograd Soviet**. This organisation issued Order Number One, which stated that soldiers need not obey any orders from the Duma-based Provisional Government that had not been agreed by the Soviet. This, then, was a period of dual authority.

- As its name suggests, the Provisional Government was temporary – it assumed responsibility until elections could be held. However, this was difficult to organise while the war continued. Meanwhile, members were reluctant to make major decisions.

- Most Russians wanted an end to the war. However, Kerensky realised that Russia needed support from the Western allies, and that it was important for Russia to continue fighting on the Eastern Front to take pressure off France and Britain on the Western Front. He hoped Russian victories would restore morale.

- The peasants demanded land from landlords – the nobles and the Church. However, the Provisional Government needed to keep support from the influential groups in Russian society, and no decision about the land was made. Meanwhile, many peasants seized the land for themselves, and this process encouraged many peasant soldiers to desert their place in the army to gain their share.

- The economic situation got worse; inflation continued. Shortages and levels of starvation only eased slightly because of the summer season.

> **Key terms**
>
> **Petrograd Soviet:** a workers' and soldiers' council.

> **Did you know** ??????
>
> The Petrograd Soviet had 3,000 members and each member represented up to 1,000 workers or soldiers. Soviets had first sprung up in the unsuccessful 1905 revolution against the Tsar. In spring 1917, Soviets sprang up in many cities and towns across Russia.

66 *It inherited nothing from the Tsar except a terrible war, a shortage of food, a paralysed transport system, no money and a population in a state of furious discontent.* 99

Alexander Kerensky writing after the Bolsheviks had taken over later in 1917

A *The problems facing the Provisional Government*

The failures of the Provisional Government

In addition to the problems inherited by the Provisional Government, its members increasingly struggled during the spring and summer of 1917.

As well as the many supporters of the Tsar, there were revolutionary parties who found it easier to make their policies known with the easing of censorship restrictions. It was not obvious at the time, but it was the small Bolshevik Party that posed the biggest threat. Its leader, Lenin, returned in April 1917 from exile in Switzerland. The German government provided a special train to take him to Russia via Sweden and Finland. The Germans hoped that Lenin would cause chaos and reduce Russia's war effort.

When Lenin arrived at the Finland Station in Petrograd, he surprised even the Bolsheviks by reading out what has become known as his April Theses. This was his plan of action for the Bolsheviks, calling for the overthrow of the Provisional Government. His famous slogans included 'All power to the Soviets' and 'Peace, bread and land'.

The Provisional Government faced a major crisis in July 1917. There were large but disorganised demonstrations against the government, led by soldiers and sailors, often with Bolshevik support. Kerensky crushed the demonstrators and 400 of them were killed. Leading Bolsheviks were arrested. Lenin fled and went into exile again, this time over the border into Finland.

In September 1917, the new Commander-in-Chief of the army, General Kornilov, decided to seize control. He wanted to restore discipline, destroy the Petrograd Soviet and gain control of the Provisional Government. His right-wing views appealed to many of the middle and upper classes. He ordered his troops to march on Petrograd. Kerensky was desperate and, in order to have sufficient troops to defend the city, he armed the Bolshevik 'Red Guards'. This succeeded, and the Bolsheviks were hailed as saviours. They kept the weapons that Kerensky had loaned them!

> **Did you know** ??????
>
> The April Theses were a series of directives for other Bolsheviks to rise up and take power. They were influential in the July Days and October Revolution.

> **Did you know** ??????
>
> The Red Guards were armed factory workers. First formed in 1905, they reappeared in March 1917 to defend the temporary government after Nicholas II was overthrown. It is estimated that by the end of the revolution there were 7,000 Red Guards in Russia.

Key profile

Alexander Kerensky

Kerensky (1881–1970) became Prime Minister of the Provisional Government in July 1917. He had trained as a lawyer and had supported the SRs. After the overthrow of the Provisional Government, he fled to the USA. He wrote books that explained, from his point of view, what had happened in Russia in the early 20th century.

B *Alexander Kerensky (left)*

Activity

1   Using pages 16–17, copy and complete the table below.

Problems faced by the Provisional Government	What it did about them (if anything)	What it didn't achieve

The growth of the Bolshevik Organisation in summer/autumn 1917

In November, Lenin and Trotsky, the leaders of the Bolsheviks, overthrew the Provisional Government. This was partly due to the weaknesses and failures of the Provisional Government. But it was also due to the way in which the Bolsheviks grew in strength in the summer and autumn of 1917. Without this, there would have been no communist revolution.

Lenin had devoted his life preparing for a revolution against the Tsar's government. He had been disappointed by the lack of progress; traditional loyalties in Russia remained strong in spite of appalling living conditions suffered by many. However, Lenin saw the First World War as a capitalist war – that is, a war between rival privileged groups, with the workers being used as cannon fodder. Following Russian defeats, discontent grew among soldiers and civilians. In spite of this, Lenin became frustrated living in exile in Switzerland and actually wrote in December 1916 that he did not expect to live to see the revolution take place! News of the unexpected and sudden abdication of the Tsar encouraged him to return to Russia, but he found the Bolsheviks numerically small and lacking ambition.

On his return, Lenin committed the Bolsheviks with his April Theses to overthrowing the Provisional Government. In May 1917, a Bolshevik Party Congress was held in Petrograd. A nine-man committee was set up under Lenin to represent the 80,000 Bolshevik Party members. Although the party had trebled in size since March 1917, it was still miniscule compared with the total population of the Russian Empire. Its agreed policies included all power to the Soviets, an end to the war, land to the peasants and the workers to control the factories.

Task

1 'Lenin was a dedicated revolutionary who did not mind if he failed.'

Do you agree? Explain your answer.

C Vladimir Lenin

Key profile

Vladimir Lenin

Lenin (1870–1924), born Vladimir Ilyich Ulyanov, was the son of a primary school teacher. He became a dedicated revolutionary after his elder brother had been executed for being involved in a plot to assassinate the Tsar. He became the leader of the Bolsheviks in 1903. He wrote many books and pamphlets whilst living and studying in Western Europe.

In July 1917, unrest in the streets boiled over into riots and demonstrations, and many Bolsheviks were involved in this, though it was not an organised rebellion and the Bolshevik leaders were not encouraging it. After the riots had been quelled and order restored by the Provisional Government, the Bolsheviks appeared weaker. Their newspaper, *Pravda*, was closed down and the Bolshevik leaders went into hiding. Lenin fled to Finland. Many anti-Bolsheviks were openly accusing him of causing the troubles, and alleged that he had been paid to do so by the German government.

However, events moved on rapidly, especially after the failure in July of the Russian offensive against Austria. Discontent again increased as the Provisional Government was seen to be weak and lack authority. Trotsky officially joined the Bolsheviks at this time.

In September, General Kornilov, Commander-in-Chief of the army, decided that, in order to win the war, drastic action was necessary. With the support of many army generals, he decided to march to Petrograd and seize control from the Provisional Government. Kerensky needed help in defending the city, so he released Bolshevik leaders from jail and helped to arm their Red Guards. The Petrograd Soviet took charge and the Bolsheviks persuaded many of Kornilov's men to desert. Kornilov's attempt failed and Lenin's Bolsheviks were seen as the saviours of Russia.

Russia was descending into chaos. More and more peasants were seizing land; more and more soldiers were deserting from the army. The Bolsheviks gained control of the Petrograd and Moscow Soviets – and others too in various parts of the country. The Bolsheviks were still very much a minority party, but they had key support where it mattered – among the workers in the cities and towns and among the soldiers in the army.

> **Did you know** ??????
>
> *Pravda* means 'the truth'. The newspaper started in 1912 in Vienna, Austria and moved to Moscow in 1918.

> **Key profile**
>
> **Leon Trotsky**
>
> Trotsky (1879–1940) was a Russian Jew who became a dedicated revolutionary. In 1903, he opposed Lenin and joined the Mensheviks, spending most of his time in Western Europe discussing and writing books. In 1917, he joined Lenin and the Bolsheviks.

D *Leon Trotsky*

The Bolshevik uprising

In October, Lenin secretly returned to Petrograd from Finland to attend a meeting of the Central Committee of the Bolshevik Party. He persuaded the committee to support a planned Bolshevik uprising. The Petrograd Soviet set up a Military Revolutionary Committee that organised the planning of the operation, led by its Chairman, Trotsky.

By early November, this had gained support from the Petrograd garrison. Kerensky knew that the Bolsheviks were planning a takeover. He closed Bolshevik newspaper offices and recalled detachments of Russian troops from the war. However, the Provisional Government had little support from the people living in the city.

During the night of 6 November, the Bolsheviks gained control of the Peter and Paul Fortress, the Telephone Exchange, power stations, railway stations, banks and main bridges in Petrograd. By the afternoon of 7 November, only the Winter Palace remained outside Bolshevik control, and that is where the Provisional Government was meeting. Kerensky, however, had fled the city in order to try and gain the support of loyal troops. In the evening of 7 November, the cruiser *Aurora*, moored in the River Neva, and under Bolshevik control, fired shells in the direction of the Winter Palace. The Red Guards attacked the palace and met little opposition – it was being guarded by a women's battalion and some trainee cadets. The Provisional Government surrendered.

Did you know ??????

The Peter and Paul Fortress was founded by Peter the Great on 27 May 1703, which is now marked as St Petersburg's City Day. The fortress housed part of the city's garrison and also famously served as a high security political jail – among the first inmates was Peter's own rebellious son, Alexei.

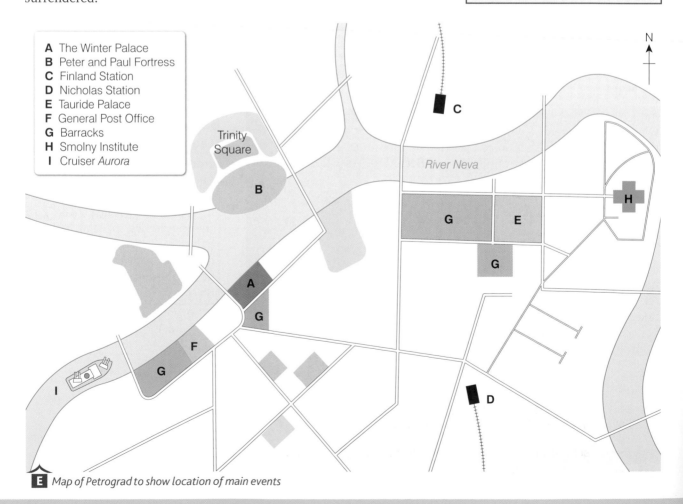

A The Winter Palace
B Peter and Paul Fortress
C Finland Station
D Nicholas Station
E Tauride Palace
F General Post Office
G Barracks
H Smolny Institute
I Cruiser *Aurora*

Trinity Square

River Neva

N

E *Map of Petrograd to show location of main events*

Early on 8 November, Lenin announced to the All-Russian Congress of Soviets that the Bolsheviks had taken over the government of Russia from the Provisional Government. In the following week, the Bolsheviks gained control in various other cities, including Moscow.

> 66 *The Provisional Government is overthrown. The Petrograd Soviet of Workers' and Soldiers' Deputies is in charge.*
>
> *The ending of the war, peasant ownership of land and workers' control of factories will be introduced.*
>
> *Long live the revolution of workers, soldiers and peasants!* 99

F Poster announcements to the people of Petrograd on 8 November 1917

> 66 *The Provisional Government had dwindled to a meeting of ministers in the Winter Palace. It was not overthrown by a mass attack on the Winter Palace. A few Red Guards climbed in through the servants' entrance, found the Provisional Government in session and arrested the ministers in the name of the people. Six people, five of them Red Guards, were casualties of bad shooting by their own comrades.* 99
>
> Taken from Taylor, A. J. P. (1980) Revolutions and Revolutionaries

G Why the Bolsheviks succeeded, according to a historian who believed that the Bolsheviks were successful because of the weakness of the opposition groups

Once the Bolsheviks were in power, they established what they called a communist government and then started providing their version of what had happened. They described how the workers had supported the Bolsheviks in getting rid of the tyrants – first the Tsar and then the Provisional Government. This was reflected in literature, paintings and music.

Lenin and Trotsky saw the importance of the cinema. There were over 1000 cinemas in Russia by 1917 (showing silent black and white films, of course). In addition, using the railway network, there were travelling cinemas. The propaganda films attracted large audiences who wanted to know what the new communist government was going to do. The most famous film, *October*, was by the Bolshevik film director Sergei Eisentein in 1927 to mark the 10th anniversary of the revolution. The takeover of the Winter Palace was transformed into a heroic struggle between the Bolsheviks and their enemies – the Storming of the Winter Palace.

Did you know ???????

When the film *October* was made in 1927 the director used, where possible, people who had taken part in the actual event. However, in the making of the film there were more casualties than there had been in 1917. Somehow, some of the 'actors' were using live ammunition!

Tasks

2   What does Source **F** suggest about the reasons for Bolshevik success in gaining support in Petrograd in November 1917?

3   How useful is Source **G** for studying the Bolshevik takeover in Petrograd in November 1917?

1.3   How successful was Lenin in creating a new society in Russia?

■ The initial establishment of totalitarian rule

When the Bolsheviks seized control, most parts of Russia were not involved. A common reaction, both in Russia and around the world, was that the Bolsheviks would soon be toppled from power.

Lenin gained substantial support by publishing wide-ranging decrees, which:

- called on all governments involved in the First World War to open negotiations for peace
- confiscated all land belonging to the nobility and the Church in order to redistribute it to the peasants
- introduced an eight-hour working day for industry
- told local soviets to take control of factories from factory owners
- granted non-Russian nationalities in the Russian Empire the right of self-government.

Some of these had little practical effect – but they were good propaganda.

However, in the first few months, Lenin was creating a **dictatorship**. He claimed he needed to do this to protect the revolution from its enemies. He set up a Council of People's Commissars with himself as chairman to rule Russia. Gradually, the leaders of other political parties were arrested. In December 1917, a new secret police, the *Cheka*, was created to round up enemies of the State. Many were executed or sent to concentration camps. The Red Guards became the Red Army to impose military rule. The wealthy lost their money and were forced to share their large houses with groups of workers. A decree banned the use of all titles.

In January 1918, elections took place for members to be elected to a **Constituent Assembly**. This assembly was supposed to decide how Russia would be governed. However, the Bolsheviks only won 175 out of 707 members, and Lenin knew that Bolshevik rule could not survive alongside this assembly. After one day, it was prevented from meeting again at gunpoint.

By 1921, there was only one party – the **Communist Party**. The Bolsheviks had created a one-party State.

> 66 *Of all the tyrannies in history, the Bolshevik tyranny is the worst, the most destructive, and the most degrading. The atrocities committed under Lenin and Trotsky are far more hideous and more numerous than anything for which the Kaiser of Germany was responsible.* 99
>
> Winston Churchill, British Secretary of State, 1919

 A *Winston Churchill's view of the Bolsheviks*

Key terms

Dictatorship: a country, government, or the form of government in which absolute power is exercised by a **dictator**.

Dictator: a person exercising absolute power, especially a ruler who has absolute, unrestricted control in a government without hereditary succession.

Constituent Assembly: people elected from the different parts of Russia to decide on the future way Russia should be governed. The elections had been ordered by the Provisional Government just before it was removed from power by the Bolsheviks.

Communist Party: the name adopted by the Bolsheviks in 1918.

Did you know ??????

The aim of the Cheka was to investigate, stop and prosecute those involved in counter revolutionary activity. It had the power to carry out investigations, arrests, interrogations, prosecutions, trials, and executions of the verdicts, including the death penalty.

Task

1   a   Write a list of reasons agreeing with Churchill's view in Source **A**.

    b   Write a list of reasons disagreeing with Churchill's view in Source **A**.

■ The end of the First World War for Russia and the Treaty of Brest-Litovsk

One big problem for Lenin was the war. The Germans had invaded Russia and were threatening Petrograd. Lenin needed peace at all costs, and a ceasefire was agreed with the Germans. Trotsky was sent to negotiate terms. The Treaty of Brest-Litovsk was signed in March 1918.

The terms were very harsh. Russia lost 26 per cent of its population, 27 per cent of its farmland and 74 per cent of its iron ore and coal. The Ukraine, Russia's main source of grain, was also lost. Huge reparations were demanded.

The peace with Germany was very unpopular. Lenin persuaded other Bolsheviks to accept the terms on the assumption that the other workers of other countries would rise up in communist revolt. International boundaries would be irrelevant when workers had control across Europe.

The gamble paid off – but for a different reason. In the autumn of 1918, Germany was suddenly forced to retreat on the Western Front and the war ended in November 1918. German troops were withdrawn from Russia, and most of the treaty was meaningless.

Did you know ??????

The Germans were reminded of the harshness of the Treaty of Brest-Litovsk when they complained about the Treaty of Versailles signed in June 1919.

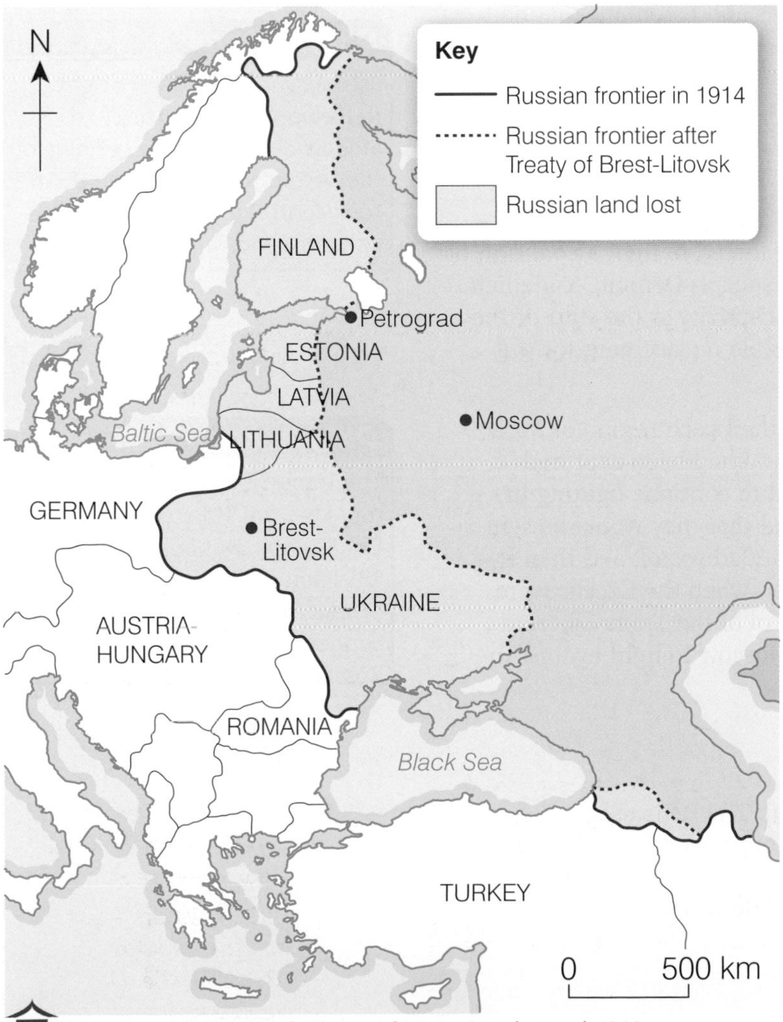

Key

—— Russian frontier in 1914

········ Russian frontier after Treaty of Brest-Litovsk

☐ Russian land lost

N

FINLAND

Petrograd

ESTONIA

LATVIA

Baltic Sea LITHUANIA

Moscow

GERMANY

Brest-Litovsk

UKRAINE

AUSTRIA-HUNGARY

ROMANIA

Black Sea

TURKEY

0   500 km

B *Map of Russia's losses in the Treaty of Brest-Litovsk, March 1918*

The causes and nature of the Civil War, 1918–21

It is not surprising that there was a **civil war**. Only a tiny minority of all the people living in the Russian Empire supported the Bolsheviks. It was, therefore, only a matter of time before Bolshevik enemies organised themselves. The problem was that it was only hatred of the Bolsheviks that held them together. The enemies included:

- other revolutionary parties such as the SRs who had much support among the peasants
- the Kadets who wanted the Constituent Assembly back to decide the future of Russia, hoping for a system of government similar to that of Britain
- landowners who had lost their land and wanted a return to the monarchy
- Church leaders who opposed the Bolshevik seizure of the extensive property of the Russian Orthodox Church, and hoped to see the Bolsheviks defeated as the first step towards recovering it
- foreign countries that wanted a government that would bring Russia back into the war, and force Germany to start fighting on two fronts again. Various countries such as the USA, France and Britain promised huge quantities of arms to the enemies of the Bolsheviks
- various national groups such as the Finns and Estonians that had been part of the Russian Empire and had won their independence at the Treaty of Brest-Litovsk in March 1918. They wanted to make sure that the new Bolshevik government did not try to take back these territories. It was because Finland and Estonia were so close to Petrograd that the Bolsheviks moved their capital to Moscow in 1918, where it has remained ever since.

Did you know

Estonia and Finland were right to be worried about their independence. At the beginning of the Second World War, the USSR took control of Estonia, Latvia, Lithuania and Finland.

Therefore, the Bolsheviks (the 'Reds') were forced to fight a coalition of 'Whites' led by former generals of the Tsar such as Denikin, Yudenich and Kolchak. The Romanov family, held in captivity at the start of the fighting, provided many Whites with a possible replacement for the Bolsheviks.

A complicating factor was the existence of the Czech Legion of 50,000 Czechs who had been fighting for Austria and had been captured by the Russians. Now, in 1918, they wanted to continue fighting in Europe against Germany. It had been agreed that they would be sent to France via the Trans-Siberian Railway to Vladivostok and then by sea – a tremendously long journey. However, when the Czechs were told by Trotsky to disarm, they seized control of the Trans-Siberian Railway and began to head back towards Moscow to fight against the Bolsheviks.

Did you know

The Trans-Siberian Railway, running from St Petersburg to Vladivostok, was built between 1891 and 1916. It covered a distance of over 9,000 km connecting European and Asiatic Russia with the Pacific Ocean.

The propaganda war

Both sides used propaganda in the Civil War. The Reds used propaganda to portray the Whites as cruel oppressors operating on behalf of foreign capitalist powers. The Reds were shown as defending Russian national interests against invading countries.

C *Bolshevik propaganda poster during the Civil War*

Trotsky used the railway network to send out travelling cinemas which showed propaganda films to the Red Army and to local people. Trotsky himself constantly toured round, using the railway network, to raise morale by making speeches. The troops were told that they were defending their country from capitalists and foreigners.

By contrast, the Whites, with less united leadership, divided aims and language barriers, failed to get their propaganda across as effectively.

The actual fighting involved brutalities on both sides. The Reds used the Cheka as well as the army. In what became known as the 'Red Terror', many people were killed, not because of what they had done but because of who they were. One Cheka leader told his men:

> 66 *Do not demand incriminating evidence to prove that the prisoner has opposed the Soviet government by force or words. Your first duty is to ask him to which class he belongs, what are his origins, his education, his occupation. These questions should decide the fate of the prisoner.* 99

Of course, the most famous victims of the Cheka were the Tsar and his family.

The Whites were just as bad. They also tortured and murdered opponents and totally innocent people. In one village, a hole was made in the ice and every villager was pushed under.

Task

2 How useful is Source **C** for learning about the role of propaganda during the Civil War? Use the source and your own knowledge to explain your answer.

⚭ links

See pages 6–7 for more information about the Tsar and his family.

See page 26 to read about the fate of the Tsar and his family.

The fate of the Romanovs

D *The bullet-damaged room at Ekaterinburg*

Soon after the start of the Civil War, the Romanov family was moved from Siberia to Ekaterinburg in the Ural Mountains. The White armies were advancing and the local Red commanders became frightened. It would be disastrous if the royal family was captured by the Whites, who could then appeal to the deep-seated loyalty felt by many of the peasants and nobles towards the Romanovs.

In July 1918, the decision was taken by local Red leaders that the family should be killed. There were 11 victims – the family and their four servants. They were taken down to the basement early one morning, the sentence of execution was read out, and a firing squad took aim. The bodies were then disposed of.

Exactly what happened has been a matter of dispute since 1918. The Reds did not want to admit the deaths. Killing a German princess would encourage a renewal of war against Germany. Killing the royal family would increase hatred toward the Bolsheviks. The local Soviet announced that they had only killed the Tsar and had taken the rest of the royal family to a safe place.

The town of Ekaterinburg did soon fall into White hands, and as a result it was White judges who investigated the disappearance. Judge Sokolov in his report in 1919 decided that all the family members were dead. The Whites were able to use this as propaganda against the murderous Bolsheviks.

Very soon after the massacre there were also stories circulating about some of the royal family escaping.

Since the fall of Communism, secret archives have been studied and, together with recent advances in DNA testing, the detailed truth has gradually emerged. In 1991, a burial pit in a bog was found containing the bodies of all the family except for Alexis and one of his sisters. Earlier this century, another pit was discovered with the remains of these two. In spite of the intrigues and romantic speculations, it was confirmed that they did all die.

Did you know ??????

Anna Anderson

Rumours of some of the family escaping were given support in 1922 when a woman in Berlin called Anna Anderson said she was Anastasia and had been rescued by a Bolshevik soldier who took pity on her. She knew intricate details of the life of the Romanov family. She convinced many people that she was genuine right up to her death in the 1970s in the USA.

Activity

1 Find out more about the detailed work that has been carried out in piecing together the evidence. See how much modern science, as well as the study of original documents, has enabled historians to declare an end to the mysteries surrounding the deaths.

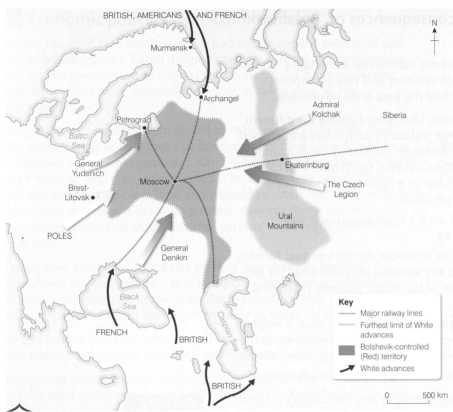

E *A map showing the advances on Moscow during the Russian Civil War*

In the north-west, General Yudenich threatened Petrograd. Indeed, by 1920, he was only a few kilometres from the city. Trotsky inspired the Red Army and Yudenich was driven back.

In the south-west, General Denikin (later replaced by General Wrangel) advanced towards Moscow, but was eventually stopped by the Red Armies.

In the east, Admiral Kolchak advanced, but his forces were defeated in 1919.

Meanwhile, the Poles (given back their status as a separate country in the Treaty of Versailles in 1919) were trying to win more territory from Russia. They were pushed back to Warsaw and forced to sign a peace treaty with the Bolsheviks in 1921.

> *Task*
>
> **3** Study Sources **F** and **G**. How useful is each source for studying the events and consequences of the Russian Civil War?

> 66 *For the first time in history the working people in Russia have got control of their country. The workers of all countries are striving to achieve this, but we in Russia have succeeded. We have thrown off the rule of the Tsar, of landlords and of capitalists.*
>
> *But we still have tremendous difficulties to overcome. We cannot build a new society in a day. We deserve to be given time. Surely the Russian people are not going to help give Russia back to the landlords, the capitalists and the Tsar?* 99
>
> *From a leaflet issued by the Bolsheviks in 1919*

F *Bolshevik propaganda in the Civil War*

> 66 *Citizens, instead of bread and peace, the Bolsheviks have brought famine and war. Russia was once a mighty country, but is now covered with the blood of peaceful citizens who are starving. The Bolsheviks are arresting and shooting workers who do not agree with their policies, and are ending all freedom.* 99
>
> *An announcement by the Whites to the workers and peasants of Russia in July 1918*

G *White propaganda against the Bolsheviks*

Economic policies: New Economic Policy

Lenin realised change was necessary, but had to persuade other leading Bolsheviks. They saw that War Communism had put into practice some of the basic ingredients of communism. Lenin had to persuade them that Russia was not ready for this. He had to change the harsh policy to win back the support of the peasants and industrial workers.

Therefore, in March 1921, the **New Economic Policy (NEP)** was introduced. It involved taking a step back from communist ideas.

I *Lenin explaining why the NEP was introduced – from a speech in 1921*

The government stopped taking surplus crops. Peasants could sell their surplus food for a profit, with the peasants paying a 10 per cent tax in kind – to be paid in crops. The government let most industry be run privately but kept control of the largest industries. Private owners were allowed to make a profit. People could buy and sell, and money became important in the economy again.

Lenin argued that the NEP should be seen as a temporary measure. The government should aim to regain control of the economy when it was more secure.

The policy worked. Production did increase.

Key terms

New Economic Policy (NEP): started by Lenin in 1921, the NEP allowed peasants some control over their land and the sale of their crops. It was introduced to get the support of the peasants, even though it went against communist theory.

Task

4 Read Sources **I** and **K** and study the statistics in Source **J**.

Do the statistics show any support for what is being argued in Source **K**? Explain your answer.

J *Production increase as a result of the NEP*

	1913	1921	1923	1925	1926
Grain (million tonnes)	80	37	57	73	77
Electricity (million kWhs)	1,945	520	1,146	2,135	2,441
Coal (million tonnes)	29	9	14	18	27
Steel (million tonnes)	4	0.2	0.7	2	3

It has been suggested that all the NEP could do was to bring the country back to the level of production just before the First World War.

> *Growth was rapid and so the system seemed to be succeeding beyond reasonable expectation. But this growth was based to a great extent on the re-activating of existing capacity. Further progress would require much greater investment effort, devoted more to building new plants than repairing and renovating old ones.*

> Taken from Nove, A. (1969) An Economic History of the USSR

K *The limitations of the NEP*

Activity

3 Draw up a table to highlight the main differences between War Communism and the NEP.

The roles and achievements of Lenin and Trotsky

The rule of Lenin was brief. In 1922, he suffered a severe stroke and also survived an attempted assassination. He became severely disabled. He died in January 1924 at the age of 54.

Lenin's achievements between 1917 and 1924 had, of course, been huge. After his death, a cult of Lenin developed. His image was everywhere – statues, posters, paintings. Petrograd was renamed Leningrad in his honour. Lenin's body was not buried but embalmed and put on display in a mausoleum in Moscow's Red Square. (Moscow had been adopted as the capital during the Civil War; it was difficult to guarantee the defence of Petrograd, and Moscow had been the ancient capital up to the end of the 17th century.)

Because of the way he was treated as a hero after his death, there is always the possibility that Lenin's achievements could be exaggerated. However, it is impossible to think of the Bolsheviks seizing power without his leadership. Lenin had kept going, usually in exile, once the Bolsheviks had been created out of the split of the Social Democrat Party. It was he who returned in the 'sealed train' from Germany to Russia in April 1917 and told the small number of Bolshevik enthusiasts to prepare for revolution. It was he who in October persuaded the Central Committee of the Bolshevik Party to organise an immediate takeover from the Provisional Government.

Trotsky had also been very much involved in the successful revolution in October/November 1917, being responsible for the actual planning of the takeover. It was Trotsky who had led the Red Army to victory in the Civil War with ruthless efficiency and organisation. It was Trotsky who organised the Red Terror during the Civil War and struck fear into the hearts of those wavering towards supporting the Whites.

Task

5 a Look back over this chapter. Write a list of activities and achievements for each of the leaders.

   b Choose **two** achievements that you think are the most important for each leader. Write a detailed answer explaining your choice.

⚭ links

See page 10 for information on the split of the Social Democrat Party.
See page 17 for more about Lenin's arrival in Petrograd.

⚭ links

See page 20 for a description of the Bolshevik uprising led by Trotsky.
See pages 27–28 to learn about the Bolshevik success.

L *A montage, made in 1920, of the leaders of the revolution. Lenin and Trotsky are together in the centre of the picture. Stalin has not been included*

M A Soviet poster produced in 1929, on the fifth anniversary of Lenin's death

Task

6 Look at Sources **L** and **M**. What can you learn about the reputations of Lenin and Trotsky just from these pictures?

AQA Examination-style questions

1   Study **Sources A** and **B** and then answer all **three** questions that follow.
In your answers, you should refer to the sources by their letters.

Source A   The Revolution of March 1917

> Most historians have concluded that the revolution was not planned. The Tsar's government seems to have collapsed because of its own weakness and the problems caused by the war. The Bolsheviks were not very active. Lenin was far away in exile. He was completely taken by surprise by the news from Petrograd.

Source B   A Bolshevik poster of 1920. It presents the slayer and the Bolsheviks (Reds) and the cowering figure as Wrangel. The text reads 'Wrangel hits again, finish him off without mercy.'

(a)   What does **Source A** suggest about the reasons for the revolution of March 1917?   *(4 marks)*

(b)   Explain why the Provisional Government became unpopular between March and November 1917.   *(6 marks)*

(c)   How useful is **Source B** for studying the reasons why the Reds won the Civil War, 1918–21?

Use **Source B** and your knowledge to explain your answer.   *(10 marks)*

Examiner's tip   In part (b), you are asked to explain why the Provisional Government became unpopular. Look back to pages 16–17. In rough, list the reasons you can find. Then try to add details to each reason. For example, the Provisional Government kept Russia fighting in the war. Then, develop this point, think what you can add about Kerensky's attack on Austria, or about the scale of suffering, or evidence about what the soldiers thought as more and more started to desert and return home. All of this, if written in appropriate English, would make this a well-developed point.

2.1

How far do the early problems of the Weimar Republic suggest that it was doomed from the start?

A *Parade of Freikorps*

Objectives

In this chapter you will learn about:

the early problems of the Weimar Republic and whether it was doomed from the start

the extent of the recovery of the Weimar Republic under Stresemann

the extent of the development of the Nazi Party up to 1929.

Key terms

Kaiser: Emperor, e.g. Wilhelm II of Germany.

Republic: a government with an elected leader rather than one that has a leader who inherits the title, such as a king or emperor.

Abdication: giving up all rights to the throne.

Fourteen Points: proposals by Woodrow Wilson, President of the USA, for a fair peace settlement that would aim to avoid future wars. The proposals were written in January 1918.

Before the First World War, Germany was a proud new nation. Until 1871 it had consisted of several independent states. By 1871 the largest one, Prussia, had managed to bring the others under its control and created a German Empire. Each of the 22 states within the empire had its own government, but the **Kaiser** (the Emperor) had enormous power. He was commander of the armed forces, decided foreign policy, and could summon and dismiss the Reichstag (the parliament). Wilhelm II had been Kaiser since 1888 and he had been determined to build up the strength of the German Empire. He had hoped that a swift victory in 1914 would achieve this. However, after four years of fighting Germany was exhausted, morale was very low, and the Kaiser was very unpopular.

Following defeat in the First World War, and the abdication of the Kaiser, Germany had to create a new government. This became known as the Weimar **Republic**. At first, it faced many problems (political, social and economic) leading to a crisis in 1923, with massive hyperinflation and Hitler attempting to seize power. Then, in the later 1920s with Stresemann as the most important politician, life improved drastically for most Germans. However, the Wall Street Crash in October 1929 brought this short-lived prosperity to an end.

The origins of the Weimar Republic

Two days before the end of the fighting in the First World War, the Kaiser **abdicated**, fled Germany and went to the Netherlands. General Ludendorff fled to Sweden. Many soldiers, sailors and workers in various towns and cities set up their own councils to govern themselves. It looked as though Germany might follow Russia in a workers' revolution.

A new government had to be formed – yet the German people were not used to democracy. Elections were held. Because of chaos in the capital city of Berlin, the new government first met in the town of Weimar in Saxony – 150 miles away from Berlin.

This period of German history (until Hitler created a dictatorship) is known as the 'Weimar Republic'. The Head of State was elected – hence the term republic – and, although after a few months the government moved back to Berlin, it kept the name of Weimar Republic.

The Armistice, 11 November 1918

The new republic sent representatives to sign the Armistice – that is, an agreement to stop fighting. The Germans believed that the peace settlement that was to be worked out would be based on the proposals of the American President, Woodrow Wilson – his **Fourteen Points**.

These gave the impression that all countries, victorious and defeated, should be treated in the same way. For example, all countries would be expected to disarm.

However, when the discussions about a peace treaty took place at the palace of Versailles near Paris, the Germans were not allowed to take part. When the terms were presented to the Germans in May 1919, they could not believe how harsh they were. Germany was to be punished, and the German leaders were told that there was no option but to sign. The French leader, Clemenceau, had wanted the terms to be even harsher.

The new Weimar government was accused of having stabbed the German army in the back by signing the Armistice. Opponents of the new government referred to the government as 'the November criminals'.

Timeline

Key events, 1918–29

1918 Nov	The Armistice – end of the First World War.
1919 Jan	Weimar Republic created.
1919 Jun	Treaty of Versailles imposed on Germany.
1919	Spartacists attempted to seize power.
1920	Freikorps attempted to seize power.
	German Workers' Party became Nazi Party.
1923	Hyperinflation peaked.
	French invaded Ruhr.
1923 Nov	Munich Putsch.
1923–9	Stresemann became foreign minister.
	Germany recovered economically.
1924	Dawes Plan.
1925	Locarno Treaties.
1926	Germany joined League of Nations.
1928	Kellogg-Briand Pact.
1929	Young Plan.
1929 Oct	Death of Stresemann.
	Wall Street Crash in New York.

The effects of the Treaty of Versailles, June 1919

Germans were angry. Firstly, representatives had to sign in humiliating circumstances. They were led into the great Hall of Mirrors at Versailles with representatives of the victorious countries looking on in silence.

> 66 *There is absolute hush. 'Let the Germans enter,' says Clemenceau. Through the door appear six soldiers in single file. And then, on their own, come the two German representatives. The silence is terrifying. They keep their eyes away from the two thousand staring eyes. They are deathly pale. It is all very painful.*
>
> *They are shown to their chairs. Clemenceau breaks the silence, saying 'We are here to sign a Treaty of Peace.' There is tension. The Germans sign. There is relief.*
>
> *We kept our seats while the Germans were led like prisoners from the dock.* 99

Taken from Nicolson, H. (1933) Peacemaking 1919

 B *A British witness of the signing of the Treaty of Versailles*

Vengeance! German nation!

Today in the Hall of Mirrors the disgraceful treaty is being signed. Do not forget it. The German people will with unceasing labour press forward to re-conquer the place among nations to which it is entitled. Then will come vengeance for the shame of 1919.

From Deutsche Zeitung, *a German newspaper, on the date of the signing of the treaty,*
28 June 1919

C *German reactions to the Treaty of Versailles*

AQA Examiner's tip

When answering questions that ask 'How useful…', think of:

- what is in the source and whether or not it is likely to be accurate, based on your own knowledge

- what the purpose of the source was; when and why it was written; who it was designed to influence.

Germans were angry because they were blamed for the war in the so-called 'War Guilt Clause'. This was considered unfair, as all major countries had contributed to the outbreak of war – including the victorious ones. Blaming Germany also justified making Germans pay for damages, known as reparations. The sum for this was fixed later in 1921 at £6,600,000,000.

Germans were angry because their armed forces were reduced to a size smaller than that of Belgium. Only 100,000 men in the army; no tanks; no submarines; only six battleships; no aircraft; no troops on the border near France in the Rhineland. Germans would not be able to defend themselves if invaded.

Tasks

1. How useful is Source **B** for studying the events of the signing of the Treaty of Versailles?

2. How useful is Source **C** for studying German reactions to the Treaty of Versailles?

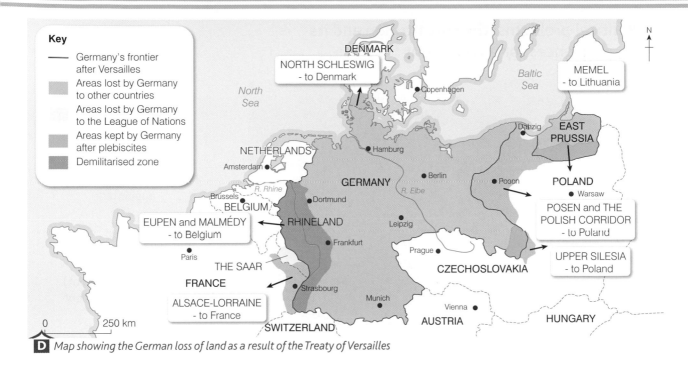

D *Map showing the German loss of land as a result of the Treaty of Versailles*

The Germans were angry because of the loss of land to other European countries. This was supposed to be justified by the principle of self-determination (one of Wilson's Fourteen Points) – that is, each nationality ruling itself. However, in many areas, different nationalities had inter-mixed over the centuries, and, when in doubt, boundaries were drawn to the disadvantage of Germans. Germany lost Alsace-Lorraine to France, part of East Prussia and Silesia to Poland, Eupen and Malmédy to Belgium, Memel to Lithuania and North Schleswig to Denmark. This amounted to over 4 million people. In addition, Germany lost all of its colonies. It was not allowed to join with Austria, which was also German-speaking.

The Treaty was to be supervised by the newly-created League of Nations, but Germany was not allowed to join.

In Germany, there were mass protests and demonstrations. Most Germans wanted to carry on fighting, but the army generals warned that there was no possibility of victory. A period of national mourning was declared.

Did you know ??????

The German people called the Treaty of Versailles the *Diktat* because it was dictated to them. They were barely allowed to negotiate any of the terms it contained and the amendments they were allowed to make were minor.

Task

3 Which **two** aspects of the Treaty of Versailles do you think angered Germans the most? Give reasons for your answer.

Political problems: the constitution and its consequences for government

E *Friedrich Ebert*

President (Head of State)
appointed

Chancellor
(Head of Government)
who needed support of

Reichstag
elected by

All adults over 20

F *Weimar democracy*

Friedrich Ebert had taken over as Germany's political leader in November 1918. He worked hard to restore order, and was determined to stop the Communists taking over.

In February 1919, Ebert became the first President of the Weimar Republic. He was a moderate, and therefore hated by both **left-wing** Communists and **right-wing** groups who wanted the army to take charge and rule in the absence of the Kaiser.

The newly-elected Weimar government met early in 1919 and agreed on its **constitution**.

The constitution was, for its time, very democratic – that is, it allowed all adults (men and women) over 20 to vote. It also allowed all of the different political parties to have a say in the government. The number of seats for each party in the Reichstag was based on the total number of votes gained by that party. This is known as proportional representation. The head of the government, the Chancellor, had to have the support of the majority in the Reichstag. Locally, each area, such as Prussia in the north and Bavaria in the south, had its own state government. The Head of State, the President, elected by all adults, was in power for a maximum of seven years.

⚭ links

See page 40 for details on the Communists (Spartacists).

Key terms

Left wing: those who believe that society should be more equal – at the extreme, Communists believing in total equality.

Right wing: those who believe in a strong country with ordinary people having little power.

Constitution: the way in which a society is governed with agreed rules.

Political instability

The Weimar Republic had political weaknesses:

- The President had the power to appoint or dismiss the Chancellor as he wished.
- The President, if he considered there was an emergency, could use Article 48 to suspend democracy for a time and rule directly with his own laws and the backing of the armed forces.
- There were many political parties and, with proportional representation, it was unlikely that any one party would gain more than half the Reichstag members – that is, gain an overall majority. This meant that there was always a coalition government. Several parties would agree to work together, thus gaining a majority in any voting. In a crisis, this did not make firm government easy.
- Among the many political parties were right-wing and left-wing factions that wanted to destroy democracy. Those parties who were more in the centre had to work hard to maintain the constitution against both extremes.
- Most judges were right wing in their views and were reluctant to deal severely with those with similar political views.

In the election of 1919, most support was for parties that were moderate or willing to join coalition governments in the Weimar Republic. However, there was also support for the extreme left-wing Communists (5.3 per cent) and right-wing Nationalists (11 per cent).

> 66 *In the event that the public order and security are seriously disturbed or endangered, the Reich president may take measures necessary for their restoration, intervening, if necessary, with the aid of the armed forces.* 99

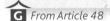

G *From Article 48*

H *Paul von Hindenburg*

Tasks

4 Why did some political groups oppose the Weimar Republic?

5 Was proportional representation a strength or a weakness in the Weimar constitution?

6 Explain both the strengths and the weaknesses of Article 48.

Challenges to Weimar, 1919–23

When war ended in November 1918, food and coal supplies were scarce and most Germans were near starvation. By 1918, Germany was producing just over half of what had been produced before the war. The allied blockade in the last two years of the war made it impossible for the German Government to import food. Many returning soldiers had no homes or jobs to go to.

During the winter of 1918–19 many suffered badly. This was made worse by the outbreak of Spanish flu, which started in summer 1918 and peaked in early 1919. More than half a million civilians and soldiers died from the epidemic.

In these economic and social circumstances, and with a new government being established, it is not surprising that there were various political challenges to its very existence.

The Spartacists

The **Spartacists** were Communists. They saw getting rid of the Kaiser as just the beginning, and aimed to copy what had been achieved in Russia in 1917 with a communist government. Some wanted to wait for the workers in Germany to become fed up with the new Weimar government; others wanted to take immediate action while there was still much unrest in Berlin.

In January 1919, some Spartacists staged an attempted revolution in Berlin against Ebert's government. However, it was badly organised and the leaders, Rosa Luxemburg and Karl Liebknecht, only supported it when it had already started.

> " *Our government does little to ensure the fair distribution of food. There is bacon in the windows of butchers' shops but the workers cannot afford to buy it. Every day 800 people die of starvation – and the children who die are not the children of the rich. For how long will such injustice be allowed to go on? The time might not be too distant when a general strike will brush away this government.* "
>
> *From the* Westphalian People's Times, *13 March 1919*

1 *Left-wing criticism of the Weimar government, March 1919*

The uprising was crushed by the *Freikorps*. Over 100 Spartacists were killed. Luxemburg and Liebknecht were captured and murdered by members of the Freikorps. In the next few months, the Freikorps put down several other communist uprisings around the country. For example, in Munich in Bavaria, a Soviet Republic was declared, copying the example of Russia. Food and clothing was taken from the rich and given to the workers. A Red Army was formed. Ebert used the Freikorps to enter the city and at least 600 Communists were killed. Altogether around the country, thousands of Spartacists were killed.

Key terms

Spartacists: Communists who took their name from Spartacus, a Roman gladiator who led a revolt in ancient Rome.

Freikorps (Free Corps): mostly unemployed ex-soldiers with extreme right-wing views and forming themselves into unofficial units.

Key profile

Rosa Luxemburg

Luxemburg (1871–1919) had been born in Poland, then part of the Russian Empire. She became a German citizen as a result of her marriage. She was imprisoned for speaking out against the First World War. She helped to found the Spartacus League, which became the German Communist Party.

Task

7 How useful is Source I for studying living conditions in Germany in March 1919? Use Source I and your own knowledge to explain your answer.

Attempted takeovers by the right-wing

The Freikorps

After the armistice in November 1918, many army officers did not want to be demobilised. Many had no jobs or homes to go to. They wanted to see Germany become a great country again and to restore German pride. They hated all Communists and those who had signed the Treaty of Versailles. They formed themselves into unofficial units, and easily found weapons and uniforms left over from the war. They were only too willing to use brutality against their declared enemies.

Ebert's new government used these army officers to help defeat the Spartacists. This gave them credibility and a self-belief in their aims.

The Kapp Putsch, March 1920

In March 1920, over 5,000 Freikorp supporters led a *putsch* and seized control of the capital, naming Dr Wolfgang Kapp as Germany's new leader for a right-wing government. The pre-1914 Imperial flag was raised in Berlin. The government fled, and called on the workers to carry out a strike in all the essential services, thus paralysing the city. The attempted putsch failed and Kapp fled abroad to Sweden.

The Munich Putsch, November 1923

The emerging Nazi Party under Hitler attempted to seize power in Munich.

> **Key terms**
>
> **Putsch:** a rebellion; an attempt to seize power.

∞**links**

See pages 49–50 for details on the Munich Putsch.

J *The Kapp Putsch in Berlin, March 1920*

Economic problems leading to hyperinflation

Prices in Germany had been rising during the First World War, and continued to do so afterwards. However, after the announcement by the allies of the reparations bill in April 1921, panic set in, leading to hyperinflation.

The invasion of the Ruhr

The first instalment of reparations payments was made in 1921, but nothing was paid in 1922. In December 1922, the German government argued that, with hyperinflation causing economic chaos, it could not afford to pay in 1923. The French thought that the Germans were exaggerating their economic difficulties to avoid paying altogether. Therefore, in January 1923, French and Belgian troops invaded Germany's main industrial area, the Ruhr, with the intention of collecting the reparations payments in kind.

The people of Germany were outraged; they were united against the invaders. The German government ordered the workers in the Ruhr to go on strike – 'passive resistance'. The French responded by sending in French workers. Germans were forbidden from leaving or entering the Ruhr without showing their passports to French soldiers. As levels of bitterness increased, sporadic violence broke out, with some Germans being shot when they refused to work. Over 150,000 German workers were removed from the Ruhr.

The strike by the workers in the Ruhr increased shortages of materials in Germany, and this further pushed up prices. The government had to print more notes to keep up. They also tried to cut down on the number of notes produced by printing larger numbers on each one. All this achieved was to send prices spiralling out of control.

 The price of a loaf of bread in Berlin, 1918 – November 1923

Date	Marks
1918	0.63
1922	163
January 1923	250
July 1923	3,465
September 1923	1,512,000
November 1923	201,000,000,000

Did you know ??????

The Ruhr exported coal to France, and imported French iron for its steelworks. Both Germany and France wanted to control the use of these resources because, together, they were worth more than they were alone. This helps to explain the French invasion of the region.

L *A German woman using banknotes to start her fire*

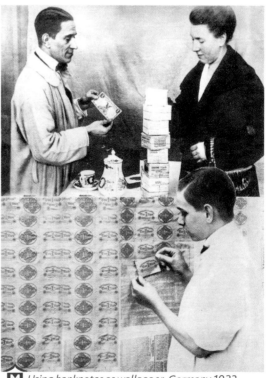

M *Using banknotes as wallpaper, Germany 1923*

Consequences of hyperinflation

Hyperinflation caused much hardship for many Germans. Those who suffered most were those living on fixed incomes, such as pensioners, or those living on savings, which became worthless. However, workers also suffered as wage rises could never keep pace with prices. Employers were forced to pay wages daily (or even twice daily) and then workers and their families rushed out to buy things before prices increased a lot more.

However, those who had debts or who had taken out loans benefited, as they could pay the money back at a tiny fraction of the original cost. Landowners were also protected from the worst of the effects, and those dealing in foreign currencies could benefit. Many rich businessmen were able to take over smaller companies that had gone bankrupt.

In the longer term, the real losers were the middle classes with businesses and savings destroyed. There was also great damage to the reputation of the Weimar Republic.

> *Germany is teeming with wealth. She is humming like a beehive. The comfort and prosperity of her people absolutely astound me. Poverty is practically non-existent. And yet this is a country that is determined that she will not pay her debts. They are a nation of actors. If it wasn't for the fact that the Germans are without a sense of humour, one might imagine the whole nation was carrying out an elaborate practical joke.*

The Times, *18 April 1922*

N *A British view of the German economy in April 1922*

> *The Weimar Republic was burdened with economic problems arising from the war. Defeat left her saddled with a huge internal debt of 144,000 million marks, and with a currency which had lost over one-third of its pre-war value.*

Taken from Carr, W. (1972) A History of Germany

O *Another British view of the German economy in the early 1920s*

Did you know ???????

During the period of hyperinflation, one man took his stack of banknotes on a wheelbarrow to a shop and left them both outside. When he came out to collect the money, he found the notes neatly stacked on the pavement, but there was no sign of the wheelbarrow. That was worth more than the banknotes and could be used for bartering.

Did you know ???????

A man stopped at a café in Berlin in 1923 to have a cup of coffee, listed as costing 5,000 marks. By the time he had paid the bill before leaving the café, the price had gone up to 8,000 marks.

Task

8 Which of Sources **N** and **O** do you think is more reliable? Use both sources and your own knowledge to explain your answer.

How far did the Weimar Republic recover under Stresemann?

■ The role of Stresemann, as Chancellor and then foreign minister

Stresemann was Chancellor from August to November 1923, and then was foreign minister until his death in October 1929. He was responsible more than any other politician for the rapid recovery of the German economy in the late-1920s, and for Germany being trusted by other countries in trade and diplomacy.

■ The recovery of the economy

New currency

In September 1923, Stresemann called off passive resistance in the Ruhr and resumed reparations payments. A new currency, the *Rentenmark*, was introduced and the old currency was scrapped. The government was becoming more stable, and the attempted putsch in Munich, led by Hitler, was defeated. French and Belgian troops were withdrawn from the Ruhr during 1924.

The Dawes Plan, 1924

A new reparations scheme was agreed. An American banker, Charles Dawes, headed a special committee to investigate the problem of German reparations. He drew up a plan that was accepted by the US government. Large American loans (totalling 800 million gold marks) were to be made available to help the German economy recover by building new factories, which would provide more jobs and wealth. Payments of reparations would be on the basis of what Germany could afford. For the first four years, smaller amounts would be paid, becoming larger as the German economy recovered.

The Young Plan, 1929

This was intended to help Germany further by extending the time period for reparations payments until 1988. It also reduced the amount Germany was required to pay to £2.2 billion.

Nationalists in Germany opposed both plans on the grounds that Germany was agreeing to pay reparations and, therefore, admitting that it had caused the war.

The intentions of the Young Plan were destroyed by the Wall Street Crash which led to the Depression. In 1932, the allies agreed to cancel reparations payments altogether. By then, Germany had paid about 12 per cent of the original reparations sum.

A *Gustav Stresemann*

∞ **links**

See pages 49–50 for details of the Munich Putsch.

Did you know ??????

Charles Dawes received the Nobel Peace Prize in 1925, in recognition of his work on the Dawes Plan.

Developments in international relations, 1924–29

As foreign minister, Stresemann worked hard to restore Germany's position in Europe as a trusted trading partner. Not all Germans were willing to follow his policy of cooperation; there was too much bitterness in the country. Stresemann was able to get support in Western European countries because they were afraid that otherwise Germany might make friends with the USSR.

In fact, Germany had secretly signed a treaty with the USSR at Rapallo in 1922. On a small scale, Germany was allowed to build factories in Russia, which produced airplanes, tanks and poison gas. All this was forbidden by the Treaty of Versailles. Stresemann aimed to develop better relations with Western Europe so that he could, in the future, make changes to the Treaty of Versailles over Poland. Poland contained a number of German-speaking areas, and the so-called Polish Corridor split Germany into two, separating East Prussia from the rest of Germany.

The Locarno Treaties, 1925

The Locarno Treaties were signed by Germany, France, Belgium, Britain and Italy. They agreed to accept the boundaries of Western Europe imposed by the Treaty of Versailles. For Germany, it meant that the French could not invade the Ruhr again. In return, Germany accepted that the Rhineland would remain a demilitarised zone. Germany and France both agreed that any future disputes would be settled through the League of Nations.

However, nothing was said about Germany's eastern boundaries – in particular, with Poland.

League of Nations, 1926

Stresemann persuaded the League of Nations that Germany should be allowed to become a member in 1926, and was given a seat as a permanent member of its Council. This was a major move away from the League being seen as a club protecting the interests of the victorious countries.

Kellogg-Briand Pact, 1928

Over 60 countries, including Germany, agreed not to use war against each other in the future. This marked the high-point of idealism in international relations in the 1920s. Memories of the horrors of the war that had finished a decade earlier appeared enduring.

However, nothing was said in the pact about what would happen if a country did not keep to the terms of the agreement.

Activity

1   Summarise:
  a   what Stresemann achieved in international relations, 1924–29
  b   the reasons that remained for many Germans still to oppose the Treaty of Versailles.

The extent of recovery in the late 1920s

Politically, the Weimar Republic appeared stable. In the Reichstag elections, extremist parties such as the Communists and the Nazis received less support than the more mainstream parties. The coalition governments that centred on the Social Democrat Party appeared to have the confidence of most of the German people.

The economy appeared to be recovering. By 1928, industrial production was greater than pre-war levels. Germany was becoming a world leader as an exporter of manufactured goods.

It was in the area of cultural activities that Weimar Germany was most obviously prosperous. The strict censorship of pre-war Germany was removed. Berlin rivalled Paris as the cultural capital of Europe. Germans led the way in innovative painting, architecture and design. Some artists, like George Grosz, used art to criticise society. He had joined the Communist Party in 1918, but his paintings do not show optimism about the chances of communist success.

Architecture and design were heavily influenced by the Balhaus movement led by Walter Gropius. He used bold designs and unusual materials with distinctly odd results. Germany also became the centre for new plays and operas. The most famous playwright was Bertolt Brecht whose *Threepenny Opera* was a huge success. There were big advances in cinema technique with silent movies. The most famous novel (later made into a film with sound) was *All Quiet on the Western Front* by Erich Remarque. It described the horrors of the First World War and within three months in 1929 had sold 500,000 copies.

> **Did you know** ??????
>
> The period of relative prosperity and stability from 1923–29 under Stresemann is often referred to as the Golden Era.

> **Did you know** ??????
>
> After having spent five months in Russia and meeting Lenin and Trotsky, George Grosz left the Communist Party in 1922, because of his hatred of any form of dictatorial authority.

B *The painter George Grosz in his studio – he used art to criticise society*

However, beneath the glittery surface, there were underlying problems.

Politically, there were still opponents of the Weimar Republic and its democratic system. Many wished for a return to rule by the Kaiser. This was seen when President Ebert died suddenly in 1925. In his place Field Marshal Hindenburg, aged 78, was elected. He had been a critic of the new democracy, and in Berlin he was greeted by cheering crowds waving black, white and red flags, the colours of the old empire. Support for communism increased during this period, and the Nazis were making advances in some local elections.

Economically, Germany relied heavily on American loans, which could have been withdrawn at any time. Imports were rising faster than exports, which meant that Germany was trading at a loss. There was still substantial unemployment. As food prices fell rapidly worldwide in 1927, farmers' income was greatly reduced and this increased their debts.

Culturally, many people criticised the new artistic developments as decadent and unpatriotic. There was also a perceived decline in moral standards, as shown in the number of cabaret shows and nightclubs in Berlin. The city became famous for its transvestite parties, where men and women shared each other's clothes. Berlin was seen by many Germans in other areas of the country as corrupt and obsessed with sex.

Did you know ??????

Before Hindenburg took up the post of president, he asked permission from the ex-Kaiser, Wilhelm II.

Task

1 To what extent did the Weimar Republic recover under Stresemann, 1924–29?

C *Marlene Dietrich starred in the film* **The Blue Angel***. The story is set before the war – a university professor is obsessed with a cabaret singer called Lola*

2.3 How far did the Nazi Party develop its ideas and organisation up to 1929?

A *Adolf Hitler (seated on the far right) during the First World War in 1916*

> ■ Germany must be united with Austria and all other German speakers.
> ■ The Treaty of Versailles must be abolished.
> ■ No Jew can be a citizen of Germany.
> ■ All citizens must have equal rights and duties.
> ■ Large companies must share their profits with their workers.
> ■ The press must be censored and controlled. All non-German influences must be removed from culture and newspapers. 99

B *Extracts from the 25-Point Programme of the Nazi Party*

Task

1 Initially, the Nazi Party was a mixture of different ideas:

■ Left-wing ideas that supported the workers.

■ Right-wing ideas that supported the rulers and emphasised nationalism.

Which of the 25 points in Source **B** are left wing and which are right wing? Explain your answer.

Timeline

The early career of Adolf Hitler

1889 Born in Austria.

1907 Lived in Vienna and tried to earn a living as an artist. During this period he picked up ideas such as hatred of the Jews.

1914 Hitler joined the German army in Munich, winning medals for bravery.

1918 Hitler was badly gassed and was in hospital when the Armistice was signed. He blamed defeat on the Communists and Jews stabbing Germany in the back.

1919 Hitler, still in the German army, joined a small extreme nationalist group called the German Workers' Party, which was founded by Anton Drexler.

1920 Hitler helped to draft the party's programme. The party was renamed the National Socialist German Workers' Party (Nazi for short).

1921 Hitler became the leader of the Nazi Party. He founded the SA (Stormtroopers) to intimidate opposition groups. Some were former members of the Freikorps. They dressed in brown. Their leader was Ernst Röhm.

Hitler was convinced that he could seize power. He had the SA, whose members swore total obedience to the Nazi movement. They broke up meetings of other political parties and encouraged violence in the streets. Hitler saw how significantly the reputation of the Weimar government had been damaged in 1923 by hyperinflation and by the French occupation of the Ruhr. In August, Stresemann had called off the passive resistance in the Ruhr and had announced the resumption of reparation payments. This seemed like a humiliating climb down. Hitler also wanted to copy the success of Mussolini, a leader with similar policies, who had taken control of Italy in 1922 with his so-called March on Rome.

Hitler personally designed the Nazi flag, with its symbol the swastika. The colours of red, white and black had also been the colours of Germany's flag under the Kaiser.

In 1924, Hitler explained the significance of the flag:

> 66 *In red we see the social idea of the movement, in white the nationalist idea, in the swastika the mission of the struggle for the victory of the Aryan man.* 99

The Nazis had gained control of a newspaper, *The People's Observer*, and this allowed them to spread their propaganda wider.

The Munich Putsch, 1923

On 8 November 1923, a meeting in a beer hall in Munich was being addressed by Gustav von Kahr, the head of the government of the southern province of Bavaria. He was very right wing in his views and hated the policies of the coalition government in Berlin. A Nazi demonstration broke out. The SA surrounded the hall; Hitler, holding a revolver, announced that he was taking over the government of Bavaria and would then march on Berlin. Kahr only agreed to support him at gunpoint.

C *Nazi stormtroopers arrive in Munich in November 1923 to take part in the Beer Hall Putsch*

D *Swastika incorporated in the Nazi flag*

E *The Nazis marching into the centre of a snowy Munich on the morning of 9 November 1923*

Consequences of the Munich Putsch

In the morning of 9 November 1923, Hitler, with the support of the war-hero General Ludendorff, marched into Munich with about 3,000 supporters. However, they were met in a narrow street by 100 armed police summoned by Kahr to break up the march. A shot was fired – no one knows by whom – and then the police opened fire. Sixteen Nazi supporters and three policemen were killed. Hitler, with a dislocated shoulder, fled from the scene.

Ludendorff, Hitler and Röhm were arrested, and put on trial for treason in February 1924. Hitler used the courtroom as a marvellous opportunity for propaganda. He spoke forcefully and played on the right-wing sympathies of the judges. Newspapers throughout Germany reported the case, and many readers were impressed with Hitler's nationalist arguments, especially after the events of the previous year.

In spite of the seriousness of the charge, Hitler was sentenced to only five years in Landsberg Castle. He was treated well; he had his own room and was allowed to have as many visitors as he wanted. He only served nine months of his sentence.

Tasks

2 'Charged with treason; given five years imprisonment in comfortable surroundings.'

a Does the punishment fit the crime? Explain your answer.

b Explain why Hitler was given a lenient punishment.

> **Did you know** ??????
>
> The word 'Nazi' is an abbreviation of the party's name in German – **Na**tionalso**zi**alistische Deutsche Arbeiterpartei.

> **Did you know** ??????
>
> While he was in prison, Hitler received favourable treatment from the guards and a considerable amount of fan mail from admirers.

> **Did you know** ??????
>
> By 1928 Ludendorff had turned against Hitler. When he heard that Hitler had become Chancellor, he predicted, 'This evil man will plunge our Reich into the abyss and will inflict immeasurable woe on our nation'.

Mein Kampf

While in prison, Hitler dictated his autobiography *Mein Kampf* (My Struggle). He set out his main political ideas as well as a very selective account of his life so far.

Hitler's main political ideas

- The Germans are a superior race – especially in comparison to the Jews and the Slavs of Eastern Europe.
- Dictatorship is essential to build up the strength of Germany after the injustices of 1919.
- Communism must be destroyed.
- The German people need more *Lebensraum* (living space) in the east in order to help establish German domination.
- Germany's natural allies are Britain and Italy.

The most important decision Hitler took while in prison was to give up the idea of seizing power by force. He realised that he had to win power legally, gaining votes leading to the election of Nazis in the Reichstag.

> **Did you know** ? ? ? ? ?
>
> By the end of the Second World War, about 10 million copies of *Mein Kampf* had been sold or distributed in Germany. Every newly-wed couple, as well as every frontline soldier, received a free copy.

F *These are the most important defendants at the trial following the Munich Putsch. Hitler is third from the right. Ludendorff stands to the left of Hitler and Röhm is on the far right*

Decline in Nazi support during the Stresemann years: consolidation of Nazi organisation in later 1920s

Nationally, the Nazis had lost a lot of credibility, especially outside Bavaria in southern Germany. The party did not do well in elections during the Stresemann years.

G *The Nazi Party in Reichstag elections, 1924–28*

Date	Nazi seats in Reichstag	Number of parties with more seats
1924 (May)	32	5
1924 (Dec)	14	7
1928	12	7

However, Hitler did use these years to reorganise the party. Local branches were set up throughout Germany, and the Nazis became a nationwide party. They got support not just from the working class, but from many farmers and craft groups. By 1929, the Nazi Party had about 100,000 members.

The Nazis were still trying to appeal to the German workers, but dissatisfied workers were more likely to support the Communist Party. In the 1928 elections the Communists gained four times the number of Nazi votes. Even so, most workers in the city were happy with the way Germany was beginning to prosper in the later 1920s, and were happy to support the Weimar Republic.

In fact, the Nazis were able to gain more support from the peasants, many of whom were not sharing in the prosperity apparent in the cities. The Nazis promised to help farming if they came to power. The Nazis also praised the traditionally-based lifestyle of the peasants in comparison with life in the immoral, violent, crime-ridden cities. The Nazis gained some support from conservative people by condemning as decadent the Weimar Republic's flourishing achievements in film, art, literature and music.

During the later 1920s the SA was enlarged in size and the **SS**, a new group loyal to Hitler personally, was created. Joseph Goebbels was in charge of Nazi propaganda.

Although the Nazis had little support overall, they were well placed to take advantage of a downturn in Germany's fortunes. This, of course, happened in October 1929.

> **Did you know ??????**
>
> The gradual fading away of competitor nationalist groups benefited the Nazi Party. As Hitler became the recognised head of the German nationalists, other groups declined or were absorbed.

> **Key terms**
>
> **SS:** a group formed in 1925 as a personal guard unit for Nazi leader Adolf Hitler.

∞ links

See Chapter 5 to find out how Hitler became Chancellor.

AQA Examination-style questions

2   Study **Sources A** and **B** and then answer all **three** questions that follow.
     In your answers, you should refer to the sources by their letters.

Source A The policies of the Spartacists (German Communists)

> The struggle for real democracy is concerned with the enemies of the working people. These are private property and control over the army and justice. We demand the transfer of power to Workers' and Soldiers' Councils, the nationalisation of all property, and the reorganisation of the army so that ordinary soldiers have power.

A list of demands published by the Spartacists in October 1918

Source B An assessment of the achievements of Gustav Stresemann

> With the death of Stresemann, Germany has lost her ablest statesman. He worked hard to rebuild his shattered country and for peace and co-operation abroad. In 1923 the French were in the Ruhr, the currency had collapsed, the reparations issue was unsolved. Germany seemed to be in ruins. Then he took over and under his leadership Germany is now orderly and prospering at home; in the affairs of Europe she has an important place.

Taken from an obituary in the British newspaper, The Times, *4 October 1929*

(a)   What does **Source A** suggest about the aims of the Spartacists?   *(4 marks)*

(b)   Explain the consequences of hyperinflation in Germany in 1923.   *(6 marks)*

(c)   How useful is **Source B** for studying the achievements of
      Gustav Stresemann?

      Use **Source B** and your own knowledge to explain your answer.   *(10 marks)*

3.1 How and why did the USA achieve prosperity in the 1920s?

A *Ford Model T in an American high street in 1925*

Objectives

In this chapter you will learn about:

how and why the USA achieved prosperity in the 1920s

how far the USA was a divided society in the 1920s

why the US Stock Exchange collapsed in 1929.

During the 1920s, the USA achieved a degree of prosperity never seen before; it was the age of the Ford motor car, of jazz, of cinema, of the stock market boom, of consumerism. However, this prosperity only reached about half the population. Poor workers, including most blacks and farmers, had lifestyles that were greatly in contrast with those of the rich. Society was divided and increasingly violent through the activities of groups such as the Ku Klux Klan and of gangsters during the period of **Prohibition**. In October 1929, the so-called 'Roaring 20s' came to an abrupt end with the Wall Street Crash when stocks and shares rapidly lost much of their inflated values. Mass unemployment and the **Great Depression** followed.

Isolationism and its effects

When the First World War started in 1914 the USA stayed neutral. The war was regarded as a distant event and nothing to do with the interests of the USA. In any case, the USA in the late-nineteenth and early twentieth centuries had become the 'melting-pot' for a huge mixture of immigrants, mostly from Europe. Loyalties would certainly be divided. The USA's **Democrat** President, Woodrow Wilson, hated the idea of war.

Key terms

Prohibition: the period from 1920 to 1933 in the USA, during which the manufacture, transportation and sale of alcohol for consumption were banned.

Great Depression: the largest worldwide economic downturn that started with the Wall Street Crash in the USA in 1929.

Democrat: one of the two main political parties in the USA, the other being the Republicans.

> 66 *The peoples of the United States are drawn from many nations and chiefly from the nations now at war. Some will wish one nation to succeed in the giant struggle, others will want the other side to win. Such divisions among us would be fatal. The United States must be neutral.* 99

B *The views of President Woodrow Wilson after the outbreak of war in 1914*

However, in early 1917, when Germany in desperation started its policy of unrestricted submarine warfare in the Atlantic, the USA was forced to enter the war in defence of its own shipping.

It took a long time to train US troops and organise essential equipment, so it was only in the summer and autumn of 1918 that they played an important part on the Western Front. Even so, over 100,000 American soldiers, sailors and airmen had been killed. When the surviving troops started to return to the USA, they were greeted as heroes, but they painted a very different picture of the fighting conditions from the romanticised version popularly believed by civilians.

D US soldiers returning home, 1919

Timeline

USA, 1919–29

1920   US Senate finally rejected joining the League of Nations.

Volstead Act brought Prohibition into force in the USA.

1921   Republican President Warren Harding in office.

Immigration quota system.

1922   Fordney-McCumber Tariff.

1923   Calvin Coolidge took over as president.

1924   National Origins Act.

1927   First solo flight across the Atlantic by Charles Lindbergh.

1928   First 'talkies' made for cinema.

1929   Herbert Hoover became president.

1929 Oct   Wall Street Crash in New York.

> 66 *American ships have been sunk and American lives taken. We have seen the last of neutrality. We must fight for the peace of the world and for the liberation of its people, the German peoples included. The world must be made safe for Democracy.* 99

C *President Woodrow Wilson's speech to **Congress** on 2 April 1917*

Key terms

Congress: the US representative assembly, the equivalent of the British parliament. The upper house is the Senate; the lower one the House of Representatives.

American refusal to joining the League of Nations

Wilson was committed to the USA playing a leading role in policing the Treaty of Versailles through active involvement in the **League of Nations**. However, the mood of America was rapidly changing. Most Americans wanted an end to 'entanglements' in European affairs, not commitments towards keeping the peace in a divided continent.

The Republican Party argued strongly against Wilson's vision. Senator Henry Cabot Lodge led the arguments against the USA joining.

> 66 I can never be anything but an American, and I must think of the United States first . . . ˆI have loved but one flag, and I cannot share that devotion and give affection to the mongrel banner invented for a league . . . The United States is the world's best hope, but if you tangle her in the intrigues of Europe you will destroy her power for good. 99
>
> *From Senator Cabot Lodge's speech to the Senate, 12 August 1919*

E *Senator Cabot Lodge's objections to the USA joining the League of Nations*

President Wilson went on an exhausting speaking tour by train across the USA, trying to persuade the American people. His train stopped at many towns where he made many speeches, but he became exhausted and suffered a stroke the day after his speech at Pueblo, Colorado.

> 66 The arrangements of the Treaty of Versailles are just, but they need the support of the combined powers of the great nations of the world. There is one thing that the American people always rise to and extend their hand to, and that is the truth of justice and of liberty and of peace. We have accepted that truth and we are going to be led by it. It is going to lead us, and through us the world, out into pastures of quietness and peace such as the world never dreamed of before. 99
>
> *From the final part of Wilson's speech at Pueblo, Colorado, 25 September 1919*

F *President Wilson arguing in favour of the USA joining the League of Nations*

After his stroke, Wilson was a semi-invalid, but in any case the Republicans were winning the argument. In March 1920, there were not enough votes in favour in the Senate for the Treaty of Versailles to be formally **ratified**. As the League of Nations was an integral part of the treaty, it meant the USA would not join the League either.

Task

1 Why was Wilson unsuccessful in persuading the American people to support his international policy?

List a few reasons in note form, and then try to add details to each one. Write up an answer in several paragraphs.

Hint

Think about what you have learnt so far in this chapter, and link it with any study you have done of Europe in 1919. You could also investigate more about Woodrow Wilson and Cabot Lodge.

The consequences for the USA

In the 1920 **Presidential election**, Warren Harding, the Republican candidate, was elected with 61 per cent of the vote, the largest majority at that time in American history. His campaign included arguments in favour of a return to 'normalcy' – a term that he coined. However, it also defined the mood of many people who wanted life to return to what it had been like before the war. In his opening speech as president, Harding said that: 'We seek no part in directing the destinies of the world.'

The USA never joined the League of Nations, a decision that, of course, had major consequences for Europe. America resumed its policy of isolationism – that is, remaining aloof from European political commitments. Not until August 1921 did the USA officially declare the war with Germany to be over.

Duing the 1920s, relations with most European countries were not good. Many of the victorious ones resented the fact that the USA had taken so long to come to their aid in the war.

During the war, even when officially neutral until 1917, US businesses had sold armaments and food to Britain and France. The USA was able to export to areas in the world controlled by European colonial countries whilst those countries were totally focused on the war. By the end of the war, the USA had overtaken Germany in the supply of chemical products. US businesses also took the opportunity to develop new materials using plastics. The old European industrial countries took time in the 1920s to refocus on international trade, and then found that the USA had captured some of their markets.

◼ Tariff policy: the Fordney-McCumber Tariff, 1922

President Wilson's policy of encouraging free trade with the USA was ended when, in 1922, the Fordney-McCumber Tariff put high tariffs (taxes) on all foreign-made goods sold in the USA. This meant that American goods were cheaper and this helped American industries. It restored the high rates imposed before the First World War, but also included farm products. This helped to end the traditional opposition from farmers to the policy of protection. The act gave the President the power to raise or lower the rate as was thought necessary. Of the 37 times that the rate was varied, President Harding and his successor, Calvin Coolidge, raised it 32 times.

Harding was not the only American president to show a faulty understanding of economics – he stated on one occasion, 'We should adopt a protective tariff of such a character as will help the struggling industries of Europe to get on their feet.'

European countries soon retaliated by putting tariffs on American-made goods.

> **Key terms**
>
> **Presidential election:** the election of a US president happens every four years in November. The successful candidate becomes president in the following year – until 1933, March; since then, January.

> **Did you know** ??????
>
> Until 1951, a president could be re-elected any number of times. This changed in 1951 with a president being limited to two terms of office – that is, eight years.

> **Task**
>
> **2** Explain the effects of the Fordney-McCumber Tariff of 1922 on the USA's trade.

Mass production

G *'Tin Lizzies' – Model T Fords coming out of the factory in 1917*

Did you know ??????

Henry Ford reputedly said: 'Any customer can have a car painted any colour that he wants so long as it is black.' Before the assembly line, Model Ts were available in lots of colours. Now only black dried quickly enough!

Henry Ford built his first motor car in 1896. In 1903, he founded the Ford Motor Company. By 1909, he was producing the Model T, and by 1914 was beginning to use a moving assembly line. This meant that each worker had his own task to do over and over again as the conveyor belt delivered the next car in the production line. Instead of taking 14 hours, a car could be produced in 93 minutes.

In the 1920s, over 1 million Model T Fords were produced each year. The price came down whilst wages for production-line workers went up. By 1925, the price of a car was less than three months' wages for an average-paid worker.

This revolution had huge effects on the American economy and on people's lives. The jobs of 4 million people depended on the motor industry. Meanwhile, other industries were expanding rapidly, with modern production techniques and electric motors taking over from steam motors.

Industrial production almost doubled during the 1920s without any increase in the size of the workforce. The number of telephones doubled during the 1920s. Canned fruit and vegetables more than doubled in this decade. Synthetic industries also mushroomed – for example, rayon transformed the textiles industry.

H *Price of a Model T Ford*

Year	Dollars
1909	950
1913	600
1917	360
1928	290

I *Cars on the roads in the USA*

Year	Number of cars on the road (USA)
1910	468,000
1920	9,239,000
1930	26,750,000

Local electric light and power companies prospered; local companies became interconnected in vast regional grids; small firms merged into great utility empires. By 1930, 10 large company groups controlled 72 per cent of the country's electric power.

The construction industry boomed as a visible sign of prosperity. For example, New York gained a new skyline where 20-storey skyscrapers were replaced by 60-storey skyscrapers. Other cities copied what New York was doing.

◼ Consumer industries and advertising

J Adverts for fashionable clothes in 1920s America

Many industries used mass production techniques to produce vacuum cleaners, washing machines, cookers, typewriters and so on. There was an explosion in advertising techniques – on billboards, in mail-order catalogues, in newspapers and on the radio. New chain stores developed, such as Woolworths, with branches in most towns and cities.

By the end of the 1920s, the largest 200 corporations (companies) possessed about 20 per cent of the nation's wealth. They had almost 40 per cent of business wealth. The biggest businesses became bigger as they bought up smaller businesses.

Hire purchase

Goods could often be bought on hire purchase, which meant people paid a deposit and then paid off the rest in instalments. It was also easy to borrow money from banks at relatively low rates of interest.

This led to a boom in sales, which increased demand in the factories, producing more jobs and higher wages, which in turn fuelled the upward spiral. As long as wages went up, people could afford to pay back what they owed.

Share purchase; the stock market boom

Companies could sell shares on the Stock Exchange in order to raise money for investment. The shares were eagerly bought by investors – who then hoped to sell them at a higher price and so make money for themselves. Therefore, in the 1920s, share prices went up, on average, by about 300 per cent.

Many ordinary Americans started to invest in shares as it seemed to be an easy way to make money. With more and more people buying shares, demand was going up, and so the prices of shares went up. As investors were convinced that the boom would continue, they often bought shares 'on the margin' – that is, they borrowed money to pay for their purchase of shares, confident that the money could be paid back as the value of the shares went up. Often banks loaned money by using the borrower's house as a guarantee. The banks themselves loaned more money than they actually had in their deposits, confident that loans would be paid back before customers wanted to withdraw their savings.

Task

3 Explain the benefits and dangers of the stock market boom.

K Traders on the floor of an American stock exchange in the 1920s

The governments of the 1920s encouraged these policies, with low taxes and little interference in business activities. They believed in 'laissez-faire' – that is, letting business leaders get on with their primary job of making money – and 'rugged individualism' – that is, making individuals responsible for their own lives and not expecting the State to do this for them.

> **Did you know** ??????
>
> The term 'laissez-faire' is a French phrase meaning literally 'allow to do'.

Tasks

4   List the reasons for the boom in the American economy in the 1920s.

5   Construct a diagram entitled 'The Cycle of Prosperity' to show how the ingredients were inter-related.

Developments in entertainment industries

In the 1920s, many people, especially whites, were better off, and they had more leisure time than their predecessors. They spent a lot of money on entertainment and, in so doing, stimulated industry and business. It was all part of the 'Roaring 20s'.

Jazz became popular. It had developed out of ragtime and blues music among black people in the southern parts of the USA. It rapidly spread throughout the USA in the 1920s and provided black musicians with a way of gaining self-respect and admiration. Jazz clubs developed, and they were frequented by the young and those wanting to shake off old traditions. The Cotton Club in New York became a famous nightclub. Black musicians such as Duke Ellington and Louis Armstrong became famous.

> **Did you know** ??????
>
> The development of electric lighting was another factor that made social entertainment more comfortable after dark, thereby popularising dance halls and live music.

Jazz style could also spread easily in the 1920s because of the availability of the radio and early gramophone records. By 1929, over 10 million homes had a radio, and local and national commercial stations were set up.

Radio stations helped to increase the popularity of sports such as baseball, boxing and American football. Some became heroes, such as the boxer Jack Dempsey. People had more money and time to go and watch sports, and, of course, with the increased ownership of cars, the possibility of travelling to watch matches.

New dances became fashionable. The Charleston, the tango and the Black Bottom became popular among the young. The dances were sexually suggestive, and frowned on by many of the older generation.

The 1920s was also a period of new crazes. Couples took part in dance marathons; doing stunts such as climbing up the outside of a tall building; or trying to break the record for sitting on the top of a flagpole. In 1927, Charles Lindbergh became an American hero by being the first man to fly solo across the Atlantic.

> **Did you know** ??????
>
> A man named Shipwreck Kelly sat on the top of a flagpole for 23 days and 7 hours. Others tried to beat the record, but failed.

The cinema

The most glamorous aspect of the Roaring 20s was the cinema industry. By 1929, going to the movies had become a national habit and 110 million people were going to the cinema each week. Before the late-1920s, the films were silent, with captions to tell the story outline. Actors needed to convey emotions through body language, and this is where some excelled – such as the sad faces of Charlie Chaplin, Buster Keaton and Harold Lloyd, and the glamorous figure of Rudolf Valentino, who gained many female fans. Some films had romantic storylines; many were comedies with slapstick humour that worked visually on screen. Cinemas employed piano players to provide appropriate background music for each scene of the film – a skilled job!

Most of the film studios were centred in Hollywood, a suburb of Los Angeles. It had a mostly dry and sunny climate and was close to both mountain and desert scenery. Big film companies developed, such as Warner Brothers, Paramount and MGM. They had large publicity departments that highlighted their star actors and actresses.

The first 'talkie' was in 1927 when Al Jolson starred in *The Jazz Singer*. After this, the silent screen stars tried to adapt their skills to the new era, but many failed to make the transition successfully because their voices were unattractive and did not match their existing 'silent' reputation.

M *Rudolf Valentino and Vilma Banks in* The Son of the Sheik, *1926*

Did you know ??????

When the first Oscars were awarded on 16 May 1929, Charlie Chaplin received a special award for his film *The Circus*. The other film to receive a special award that year was *The Jazz Singer*.

L *Charlie Chaplin in* The Kid, *1921*

Did you know ??????

Rudolf Valentino died in 1926, aged 31, of appendicitis. People queued for hours to see his embalmed body and thousands attended his funeral.

Activity

1 Try to watch at least one silent movie of the 1920s. Analyse how the producers and the actors ensure that the audience remains interested without any speaking.

3.2   How far was the USA a divided society in the 1920s?

Rich versus poor

The 1920s was a decade of contrasts, particularly between the tremendous wealth of some groups and the extreme poverty of others. In early 1929, about one-third of the nation's wealth was shared by only 5 per cent of the population. The national income of the USA was bigger than that of Britain, Germany, Japan, France and 18 other countries put together.

Blacks made up about 10 per cent of the population, most of whom lived in squalor and misery, and were generally seen as an inferior race. Many still lived in the south; the states of Mississippi and South Carolina were mostly black. Living conditions in the remote cotton-growing areas were appalling – especially in comparison with growing wealth elsewhere. Many blacks suffered at the hands of the Ku Klux Klan.

Poor immigrants who were not white North Europeans were seen as a threat to both American culture and to living standards. Native Americans existed, but mostly on reservations in various parts of the USA.

Some predominantly white groups did not benefit much from the boom years either. Workers in the old industries of northern USA were exploited with bad working conditions and low wages. These included shipbuilding, textiles and coal mining.

In 1929, 71 per cent of American families had annual incomes under $2,500. This was generally believed to be the minimum needed for a decent standard of living. Children were also exploited in textile mills and in agricultural work. Up to 2 million 14–15 year olds worked in these occupations for up to 11 hours per day for very low wages.

Farmers struggled because of overproduction and consequent low prices. During the First World War, demand had been high for food exports to Europe. However, in the isolationist atmosphere of the 1920s, with tariff barriers and more competition, many farmers fell into debt and lost their land. New synthetic fibres such as rayon reduced the demand for cotton. Many farmers experienced the Great Depression several years before the Wall Street Crash.

∞links

See pages 64–66 for information about the Ku Klux Klan.

Did you know ??????

Native Americans who were not already US citizens as a result of other agreements were granted citizenship in 1924 by the Congress of the United States.

Task

1   Draw two spider diagrams – rich and poor. For each, choose what you think are the five most important facts from this page.

Activity

1   Research further the divisions within American society in terms of wealth and poverty. You could watch the film *The Great Gatsby* to see an example of the extremes of wealth.

Race: immigration controls

Before the First World War, the USA had no restrictions on immigrants and had become the 'melting-pot' of races and nationalities. There were more religions and more languages in the USA than in any other country.

However, some Americans were alarmed at the growing number of immigrants in the swelling cities. In the 25 years before 1914, the vast majority of immigrants were coming from Southern and Eastern Europe. Mostly Catholic, they spoke languages that seemed bewildering in the eastern states that mainly spoke English or German. Overall, there was a growing feeling that these recent immigrants were inferior and less educated. It was a form of racial prejudice.

In 1917, a law was passed that imposed a literacy test on immigrants. This favoured those from Northern and Western Europe – mostly whites and mostly Protestant. However, this law was fairly ineffective and, after the war ended, there were fears that millions of Europeans would flood to the USA.

In 1921, Congress passed the Emergency Quotas Act. Quotas were based on nationality. The number of people admitted into the USA in any one year was limited to three per cent of all the emigrants from that country who were resident in the USA in 1910. This favoured countries in Northern and Western Europe again, as these were the people who had emigrated in the largest numbers over the previous 200 years.

In 1924, the National Origins Act was passed. This put further restrictions on immigration. The three per cent figure was reduced to two per cent, and the year of residency moved back to 1890. This was significant as in the quarter-century before the First World War there had been a huge increase of immigrants from countries such as Italy, Russia, Turkey and Greece. The overall number of European immigrants was to be restricted to 150,000.

This was reflective of the overall mood of isolationism among many Americans in the 1920s.

Activity

2　Imagine what it would be like arriving in New York from Europe in the 1920s.

List the problems you would probably be facing in the first few weeks. Then, with a partner, discuss how you would go about solving these problems.

Race: the Ku Klux Klan

Black Americans in the early 20th century

Although blacks had gained their freedom from slavery in the 1860s, they still suffered badly from racial discrimination. **Segregation** was legal in the southern states where most blacks lived and worked. Blacks usually had the worst jobs and houses, could not eat and travel with whites, and could not expect fair treatment in the courts where the judges were always white. In some states, marriage between blacks and whites was forbidden.

Key terms

Segregation: the policy of keeping different races apart.

In 1896, the **US Supreme Court** had given legal approval for what became known as the **Jim Crow laws** – that is, treating blacks as inferior people. White southerners could protect their way of life and continue to exploit those who they believed to be racially inferior.

In the 1920s, with the industrial expansion in the USA, nearly 1 million people left the south of the USA to migrate to the north where there were jobs available in the expanding cities, including work in factories. Conditions were a little better there, but there was still much racial discrimination. Blacks were the lowest paid and the first to lose their jobs. Black neighbourhoods, known as ghettos, grew up in some cities such as New York.

A *A Ku Klux Klan parade in Washington DC, 1925*

Key terms

US Supreme Court: the highest court in the USA, made up of nine judges who decide on disputed points of law.

Jim Crow laws: Jim Crow was a character in an old song that was made popular by a white comedian who made fun of the Black Americans. Jim Crow became linked to a series of laws that were passed by the southern states to discriminate against the Black Americans living there. The laws segregated them from the whites and kept them as second-class citizens.

Did you know ??????

Black American voting rights were restricted or denied through suffrage laws, such as the introduction of poll taxes and literacy tests, while loopholes protected the rights of white people who were unable to pay the tax or pass the test.

Did you know ??????

Although slavery had been abolished, many black workers continued to 'sharecrop'. The planters could not afford to pay wages to the former slaves, but instead lent them plots of land to work in return for a percentage of their crops.

1 Why did the US Stock Exchange collapse in 1929?

Write an essay taking into account all the reasons – both short and long term. This will involve the problems that had been building up in the 1920s, as well as the events of October 1929. Your task is to explain the reasons, not merely describe events.

2 Despite prosperity for many during the 1920s, the seeds of the 1929 economic disaster were being sown. Review this chapter and use the notes below to work out the main problems of the 1920s and why the 'boom' could not last for ever.

Write a paragraph, with details/examples, for each of the problems:

a Some traditional industries and farming were not thriving. Many Americans were not sharing in the prosperity and there was an unequal distribution of wealth. See page 63.

  i What did this suggest about the ability of these people to keep buying new goods? Give examples.

  ii What effect would this have eventually on economic growth?

b The success of mass-producing goods was leading to overproduction. See pages 58–59.

  i What would this mean for the companies producing too many goods?

  ii What would this mean eventually for the workforce in these companies?

c The foreign trading position of the USA was unhealthy with the effects of the tariff policy. See pages 57 and 63.

  i What did the USA do to discourage imports?

  ii What did other countries do in retaliation?

  iii What effects would this have on the USA trying to sell more goods?

d Many small banks had gambled too much with their customers' money. See page 60.

  i What did the banks do that assumed that the boom would continue indefinitely?

  ii What would this mean if stock market prices went down?

e Big businesses had borrowed heavily in order to expand. There was insufficient credit control.

  i How would businesses be affected if sales went down?

f The huge rise in the value of shares had led to increased speculation and significantly more people buying 'on the margin' (only paying for part of the share purchase and taking out a loan to pay the rest), confident that prices would continue to rise. See page 60.

  i What would this mean if and when share prices started to fall?

  ii What would happen to those who had speculated on the market and owed huge sums of money?

g Finally, which do you think was the most important problem? Explain your choice carefully.

AQA Examination-style questions

3   Study **Sources A** and **B** and then answer all **three** questions that follow.
In your answers, you should refer to the sources by their letters.

Source A American attitudes towards the world after the First World War

> Many Americans did not share President Wilson's idealism. Public opinion had become strongly isolationist. Americans had no wish to get involved in world problems, and European conflicts in particular. They did not want to have to pay for the cost of keeping world peace. Warren Harding, the new President, won the election of 1920 by promising to put America first.

Source B The front cover of the Sears, Roebuck and Co. catalogue, 1927

(a)   What does **Source A** suggest about why the USA did not join the League of Nations?   *(4 marks)*

(b)   Explain the consequences of Prohibition in the USA in the 1920s.   *(6 marks)*

(c)   How useful is **Source B** for studying living standards in the USA in the 1920s?
Use **Source B** and your own knowledge to explain your answer.   *(10 marks)*

The cult of personality

During the 1930s, Stalin increasingly used his control of the government to present himself in a favourable light. The image he created of himself was a caring, friendly leader.

Writers, film-makers and artists were told that they must produce works in praise of Stalin's achievements. History was re-written to give Stalin an important role under Lenin in the early days of communism. Dissenters were punished, such as the writer Solzhenitsyn, who criticised Stalin's rule and was sentenced to 8 years in one of Stalin's labour camps. Musicians were expected to compose popular pieces celebrating the achievements of the Soviet workforce in the modernisation of the country.

Propaganda posters featuring Stalin and happy Russian workers were common. Visual images helped to spread the desired message of happy workers striving for success.

E *Stalin and adoring crowds – this montage dates from the late 1930s*

Task

4 How useful is Source **E** for studying Stalin's position in the USSR in the 1930s? Use the source and your knowledge of the period to explain your answer.

Labourers at work. This is a propaganda poster produced in the 1930s. Note the anvil to symbolise industrial work. The hammer and sickle at the bottom are used to represent the USSR. 'We have destroyed the enemy with weapons, we'll earn our bread thanks to our work. Pull up your sleeves comrades!'

Task

5   What can you learn from Source **F** about propaganda in the USSR in the 1930s?

Dmitri Shostakovich, the Russian composer

Shostakovich (1906–75) had been brought up in the USSR under communist rule. He was proud to be Russian, but hated the excesses of communist dictatorship. However, he had to be careful how he expressed himself in music if he wanted to escape criticism and punishment. Sometimes, when he was trying to express personal emotions, he used a four-note motif using the letters DSCH. (D comes from his first name, Dmitri, and SCH are the first three letters of his second name as spelt in German). Using German notation, D is D, S is E flat, C is C and H is B natural. Play this on a keyboard – or get a friend to do it for you. These four notes appear frequently – sometimes quietly and slowly; sometimes with great force and anger. To hear a good example of this, find a recording of his Tenth Symphony and listen to the short second movement. It is very explosive and angry in character.

A closer look

To what extent did Stalin make the USSR a great economic power?

■ The economic situation in the USSR in the late-1920s

Lenin had introduced the NEP in 1921, it allowed peasants to own their land and sell any surplus food. The system provided incentives for more food to be produced. Some peasants – the kulaks – became quite well off. Some of the kulaks employed other peasants to work on their land. Many of these peasants resented the more privileged position of the kulaks.

Despite food production increasing in the 1920s, there were fundamental problems that limited this growth. The peasants who owned their small plots of land were using mostly primitive methods of agriculture with little machinery and low yields. Furthermore, there was very little industrial development considering the size of the country. The USSR was vulnerable to attack from Europe, as it had been in 1914 and in previous centuries. The country urgently needed more industry to produce weapons. But if more people were to work in factories and live in cities, much more food would have to be produced to feed the industrial workers. In addition, the USSR would need to buy machinery needed for industrialisation from abroad, and this could only be paid for through the export of food.

Therefore, in 1929, Stalin decided to abandon the NEP. New policies would mean that the State took direct control of agriculture and industry. This would ensure much higher levels of production and strengthen the position of the USSR so that it could withstand any invasion.

CO links

Look back to Chapter 1 to remind yourself about the NEP.

> **66** Do you want our socialist fatherland to be beaten and to lose its independence? We are fifty or a hundred years behind the advanced countries. We must make good this distance in ten years. Either we do it or they will crush us. **99**

A *Stalin summed up the problems facing the USSR in a famous speech in February 1931*

■ Collectivisation: the theory, the process and the results

The theory was simple – large farms would be more productive than small plots of land. This was because large farms, called collectives, could use machinery such as tractors and combine harvesters. Stalin was also aware that not many of the peasants were actually Communist Party members and was not sure if he could rely on their loyalty.

The process of collectivisation began in 1929. Twenty-five million peasant farms were to be combined to form 240,000 collective farms (called *kolkhoz*). Immediately, most peasants opposed giving up their land, and many of them killed their livestock rather than hand them over to the State. The kulaks had the most to lose. Stalin embarked on a policy of destroying the kulaks as a class. Anyone accused of being a kulak was imprisoned, shot or transported to Siberia.

The destruction of livestock had disastrous consequences. It is estimated that the animal population fell by about half in three years. This, coupled with the disruption caused by collectivisation, led to a terrible famine in which an estimated 6 million people died between 1931 and 1933.

Production levels increased in the later 1930s, but many peasants remained in extreme poverty and were always at the mercy of a bad harvest or an extra cold winter. A substantial proportion of grain was exported, and there were still many more industrial workers in the cities to be fed.

The locally controlled kolkhoz were supervised by Soviet Party officials. This was frequently necessary as the peasants had no incentive to work hard, as any surplus would be taken away from them. However, for those who did work hard, collective farms could bring benefits. Schools and hospitals were built, and peasants could feel pride in the achievements of their kolkhoz. Later, in the 1930s, Stalin allowed peasant families to have a small individual plot, with one cow and several pigs or sheep.

B Amount of grain, cattle and pigs in the Soviet Union

	1928 (millions)	1933 (millions)	1940 (millions)
Grain (tonnes)	73	69	95
Cattle	29	19	28
Pigs	19	10	27

C Propaganda poster by Josif Gromitsky: 'The aim of the production of collective farms is to crush capitalism'

The economic, political and social consequences of the plans

Despite setbacks and exaggerated claims, the USSR succeeded in substantially expanding its industry in the 1930s as a result of the plans. When the USSR was invaded by the Germans in 1941, sufficient progress had been made to enable effective resistance. The USSR transformed itself at a time when most other major countries were suffering the effects of the Great Depression, with millions out of work.

The social consequences were mixed. Millions died working on industrial projects and millions of peasant families were uprooted and forced to live thousands of miles away. Working conditions were harsh, with a seven-day working week. Accidentally damaging tools was treated as sabotage, and absenteeism or lateness was treated as a crime. Those who worked hard and succeeded were treated as heroes. In August 1935, the Soviet press announced a new hero, a coalminer called Alexei Stakhanov. It was claimed that he had mined 102 tonnes of coal in one shift – about 14 times the total an average worker could mine. Stakhanov was praised, given medals, and went around giving lectures on how to improve productivity. Those who successfully copied his achievement were called Stakhanovites.

With the rapid growth of cities, new housing could not keep pace with demand. Many had to live in dormitories. Many families lived together in one room of a flat.

On the other hand, society began a transformation. Gradually, living conditions did improve, especially in the established cities. Electricity became available for everyday use. Radios improved communications. Education was free; hospitals with free health care became available. Some blocks of flats had central heating. Those living in Moscow could be proud of the new buildings, including the Moscow underground with its spaciousness, its cathedral-style arches, colonnades and bright paintings.

The foundations had been laid for the USSR to become a superpower, which it did after the defeat of Germany in 1945. Stalin remained in power until his death in 1953. By then, the USSR controlled much of Eastern Europe and had developed an atomic bomb, making the USSR the second most powerful country in the world. Industrialisation in the 1930s was harsh, but it achieved results on a scale that no one living at the time could have predicted.

Did you know ??????

Stakhanov's achievement was resented by many Russians. What he had done could easily be regarded as the result of just hard work and, therefore, the same standard could be expected of others. Soviet workers were not told that he was given the best seam of coal to work, the most modern equipment to use, and unskilled assistants to carry the coal away for him.

AQA Examination-style questions

4   Study **Source A** and then answer **both** parts of the question that follows. In your answers, you should refer to the source by its letter.

Source A Construction of the Dnieper Dam in 1931

(a)   During the building of the dam, living conditions for many were very poor

Using **Source A** and your own knowledge, describe the effects of the Five Year Plans on the Russian people.   (*8 marks*)

(b)   'Stalin came to power instead of Trotsky because of Stalin's better leadership skills.' Do you agree? Explain your answer.   (*12 marks*)

5.1 How and why was Hitler able to become Chancellor in January 1933?

Objectives

In this chapter you will learn about:

how and why Hitler was able to become Chancellor in January 1933

how Hitler changed Germany from a democracy to a Nazi dictatorship in 1933–34, and how he reinforced this

the extent to which Germans benefited from Nazi rule in the 1930s.

A Adolf Hitler

When the Wall Street Crash happened in the USA, Hitler and the Nazis had little national support. However, as unemployment in Germany soared, so did support for extremist political parties – the Communists and the Nazis. Both promised solutions to Germany's economic and social problems. The Nazis also promised to restore Germany's pride.

In January 1933, Hitler became the leader of the largest party in the Reichstag. Within 18 months, he had become a dictator. Between then and the outbreak of the Second World War in 1939, Hitler tightened the grip of Nazi policies on the German people. Political opposition was crushed as parties other than the Nazis were banned. Nazi propaganda seeped through into every aspect of life including the education of children. The SA, SS and Gestapo (secret police of Nazi Germany) ensured that any non-Nazi expression of opinion was acted on ruthlessly. Many came to realise too late that there was a huge price to be paid for supporting a party promising to restore Germany's pride.

∞links

For details on the Wall Street Crash in the USA, see pages 72–73.

See page 22 for a definition of the term 'dictator'.

See pages 49 and 52 respectively for more about the SA and SS. Also pages 102–103 for Hitler's elimination of the SA.

The impact of the Wall Street Crash and Depression in Germany

When the American economy went out of control following the Wall Street Crash in October 1929, the economic depression quickly spread to Europe, especially Germany.

All European countries were affected by the drop in world trade and the rise in unemployment. However, Germany also suffered when American banks demanded repayment of loans given to Germany since 1924.

Many businesses in Germany went bankrupt. By 1932, almost 6 million people were unemployed. Many others suffered from the effects of low wages or part-time working; they could not afford to pay rent and became homeless.

The German government was powerless. As a result of the system of proportional representation, there were several small political parties represented in the Reichstag, but no party had more than half of the seats. Therefore, many parties had to join together in a coalition in order to get votes passed by a majority.

With life becoming very difficult for millions of Germans, many looked towards extremist solutions. Both the Communist and Nazi parties gained supporters. The Communists appealed to the poor working class. The Nazis tried to appeal both to businessmen, who had lost everything in the economic collapse, and to the unemployed workers.

The Nazis spread their ideas through posters, pamphlets and Nazi-controlled newspapers. The Nazi message was spread through simple slogans such as 'ein Volk, ein Reich, ein Führer' (One People, One Nation, One Leader).

Josef Goebbels was appointed head of propaganda within the Nazi Party in 1929. He exploited the possibilities of modern as well as older means of communication much better than the other political parties. For example, Nazi poster campaigns always targeted particular audiences; speeches at public meetings always dwelt on topics suitable for that particular audience.

Where possible, local issues were exploited. The Nazi private army, the Brownshirts (SA), threatened political opponents and encouraged an atmosphere of chaos. Meetings of other parties were disrupted, members beaten up and fires started. They blamed the Communists for the violence.

Hitler made many speeches, stressing simple facts. He had written in *Mein Kampf* that:

'The memory of the masses is very restricted and their understanding is feeble; they quickly forget. So all effective propaganda must be confined to a few bare essentials expressed in simple terms. These slogans should be persistently repeated.'

He spoke at length about the disgrace brought to Germans by the shameful Treaty of Versailles.

Timeline

Key events, 1929–39

1929	Wall Street Crash in the USA led to huge economic problems in Germany.
1932	Nazi Party did well in elections. Hitler defeated by Hindenburg in Presidential Election.
1933 Jan	Hitler invited to become Chancellor.
1933 Feb	Reichstag Fire.
1933 Mar	Enabling Act passed.
1933 spring/ summer	Political opposition to Nazis banned.
1934 Jun	The Night of the Long Knives.
1934 Aug	Hitler succeeded Hindenburg as President.
1935	Nuremberg Laws.
1936	Berlin Olympic Games.
1938	Kristallnacht (The Night of Broken Glass).
1939 Sept	Germany invaded Poland; Second World War started.

links

For details on the loans from the USA to Germany, see page 44.

Key terms

Mein Kampf: the book that Hitler wrote in prison in 1924 after the failure of the Munich Putsch. Translated, the title means 'My Struggle'.

links

For more information about *Mein Kampf*, see page 51.

The Weimar system of government

With proportional representation, Weimar Germany always had coalition governments. Groups of political parties had to join together to form a government – and often they disagreed, making effective government impossible. Using Article 48 of the constitution, the President could, in an emergency, make laws without consulting the Reichstag. This meant that he could pass laws by decree, which could be dangerous if misused. At this time, the President was the highly-respected First World War hero, General von Hindenburg. It was his job to try to establish a stable government so that solutions could be found to the economic crisis.

Between March 1930 and May 1932, the Chancellor of Germany was Heinrich Brüning, but his economic policies were very unpopular. He raised taxes, cut the level of unemployment benefit and reduced the salaries of government employees.

Meanwhile, the Nazis were growing substantially in popularity. Hitler appealed to the German people's nationalism; to their pride that had been badly dented; and to their belief that Germany had been 'stabbed in the back' by cowardly politicians after the First World War. Hitler was also quick to blame Jews for the financial ills that had hit Germany, and visual propaganda was effective in showing the Jews as greedy bankers and businessmen enjoying wealth at the expense of poor German citizens.

As Hitler became well known within Germany, he decided to fight against Hindenburg in the Presidential Elections, held every seven years. Hindenburg won with 19 million votes, but Hitler came a respectable second with 13 million votes. Hitler had used the campaign to hammer home the main Nazi messages based on the nationalism of Germans, their hatred of the Treaty of Versailles and their suspicion of the Jews.

⊂⊃ links

For a fuller explanation of the Weimar system of government, see pages 38–39.

⊂⊃ links

For more information on Article 48, see page 39.

B A Nazi propaganda poster, 1932. The words say 'Yes, Führer, we follow you'.

Task

1 How useful is Source **B** for studying why the Nazis gained so much support in the years 1929–32? Use Source **B** and your own knowledge to explain your answer.

C Number of Reichstag members elected, 1928–33

	May 1928	Sept 1930	July 1932	Nov 1932	March 1933
Communists	54	77	89	100	81
Socialists	153	143	133	121	120
Centre Party	78	87	97	90	93
Nationalists	73	41	37	52	52
Nazis	12	107	230	196	288
Other political parties	121	122	22	35	23

Hitler's appointment as Chancellor

In May 1932, Hindenburg appointed Franz von Papen as Chancellor. Von Papen was a member of the Centre Party and found he did not have enough support to rule effectively. He called a general election in July 1932, the result of which was that the Nazis gained a lot of support at the expense of the minority parties.

As von Papen needed more support, he called another general election in November 1932. This result gave him even fewer seats so he resigned and von Schleicher became Chancellor. He too failed to gain a majority in the Reichstag. Hindenburg was forced to do what he had been trying to avoid – to ask Hitler to become Chancellor. There had been increasing pressure on Hindenburg to do this ever since July 1932 when the Nazis became the largest political party, but Hindenburg despised Hitler and thought him and his party unworthy of ruling Germany. In January 1933, Hindenburg was forced to make Hitler Chancellor and even shook hands with him on his appointment. He did try to ensure that Hitler's power would be limited by making von Papen the Vice-Chancellor and restricting the number of other Nazis in the Cabinet to two.

D *Hitler being sworn in as Chancellor in front of Hindenburg and leading Nazis*

> ### Did you know ??????
>
> Von Papen was a very unpopular choice for Chancellor, and his appointment only served to increase the German people's frustration with the Weimar system of government.

Task

2   Why was Hitler able to become Chancellor of Germany in January 1933?

Write an essay in answer to this question. Include:

- the effects of the Wall Street Crash on people in Germany
- what the Nazis said to get support
- how the Nazis got their message across
- the steps to power between 1930 and January 1933, including the role of Hindenburg.

When Hitler became Chancellor, he appeared to have limited control. The Nazis did not have a majority in the Reichstag; there were only three Nazis, including himself, in the Cabinet. The Communist Party had much support, especially among the working classes. Yet, within 18 months, Hitler had destroyed the Weimar constitution and become a dictator.

The Reichstag Fire, February 1933

Hitler had called for an election to be held in early March 1933. Then, on 27 February 1933, whilst he was having dinner with his propaganda minister, Josef Goebbels, the Reichstag building was severely damaged by fire. Hitler immediately blamed the Communists. Hitler and Goebbels raced by car to the burning building. Hitler immediately declared: 'This is a signal from God. If this fire turns out to be the work of the Communists, then there is nothing that shall stop us from crushing out this murderous group with an iron fist.'

Dutch Communist Marinus van der Lubbe was caught at the scene, but it is debatable whether he was responsible. After his arrest he behaved very strangely and said very little. After 11 months he was found guilty, and having admitted his guilt, was beheaded.

The Communists and other groups gave a different version of events. They said it was all a Nazi plot so that Hitler had an excuse to blame the Communists. One story alleged that van der Lubbe may have started one of the fires, but that the SA had helped him by starting the others that all appeared to start at the same time. Some had suspicions that the Nazis started the fire themselves, especially considering how Hitler made political use of the fire.

A *The Reichstag Fire*

The day after the fire, Hitler persuaded President Hindenburg to pass an Emergency Decree using Article 48 of the constitution. This law for the 'Protection of the People and the State' gave Hitler sweeping powers to arrest anyone suspected of opposing the government. It ended all personal liberty, stopped freedom of expression, and took control of the press.

This gave Hitler the opportunity to act against his political opponents. Many of them were arrested; others were too afraid to vote because of the threatening behaviour of the SA. The SA intimidated suspected opponents, trying to force them into open opposition to the Nazis so that they could be arrested.

This gave Hitler the opportunity to act against his political opponents in the March election. Many of his opponents were arrested; others were afraid to vote because of the threatening behaviour of the SA.

Read the sources below and decide what you think about the cause of the Reichstag Fire.

∞links

See pages 34–35 for more on the Weimar Republic and the Constitution.

> 66 *I think van der Lubbe started the Reichstag Fire on his own. When I arrived at the burning building, some police officers were already questioning him. His voluntary confession made me think that he was such an expert arsonist that he did not need any helpers. Why could not one person set fire to the old furniture, the heavy curtains and the bone-dry wood panelling? He had lit several dozen fires using firelighters and his burning shirt, which he was holding in his right hand like a torch when he was overpowered by Reichstag officials.* 99
>
> From an account written in 1950 by Rudolf Diels, a Nazi and head of police in Berlin in 1933

B One view of the responsibility for the Reichstag Fire

> 66 *Göring had been looking for an excuse to smash the Communist Party. He at once declared that van der Lubbe was only part of a larger communist plot to start a campaign of terror. The burning of the Reichstag was to be the signal for communist revolt.*
>
> *In fact, I believe that the burning of the Reichstag was planned and carried out by the Nazis themselves. Van der Lubbe was picked up by the SA (the Brownshirts) after he had attempted to set fire to other buildings. He had been allowed to climb into the Reichstag and start a fire on his own in one part of the building while Nazis started the main fires.* 99
>
> Taken from Bullock, A. (1952) Hitler: A Study in Tyranny

C A second view of the responsibility for the Reichstag Fire

> 66 *The Nazis had nothing to do with the burning of the Reichstag. The young Dutchman, van der Lubbe, did it all alone, exactly as he claimed. Hitler and the other Nazis were taken by surprise. They genuinely believed that the Communists had started the fire.* 99
>
> Taken from Taylor, A. J. P. (1961) From The Origins of the Second World War

D A third view of the responsibility for the Reichstag Fire

Did you know ??????

A British reporter, who witnessed the events of the Reichstag Fire, suggested that the Communists sought to make it appear that van der Lubbe was working for the Nazis, who had plotted the whole thing.

Task

1 a Analyse Sources **B**, **C** and **D** and also investigate other versions and conclusions about the Reichstag Fire. There is no general agreement about the exact sequence of events nor the responsibility.

   b Write your own conclusions using the evidence you have found.

The election of March 1933 and the Enabling Act

"LET THE GERMAN PEOPLE DECIDE !"

E A British cartoonist's view of what the March 1933 election would be like. The notice on the polling booth reads: 'Parties opposing Hitler are severly discouraged'

Look at the statistics in Source **F**. In the election of March 1933, although the Nazis were by far the largest party, they did not have an overall majority – just 44 per cent of the seats. Hitler was therefore disappointed with the result, but he used the state of emergency declared by the President to stop the Communists from taking their seats. He won over the Centre Party with promises to protect the Catholic Church in Germany. The Nationalists were prepared to support him as well. Those arriving at the Kroll Opera House (the temporary home for the Reichstag after the fire) were ushered in by heavily-armed SA men.

The Reichstag members passed the Enabling Act, which gave Hitler the power to make his own laws without the Reichstag. Members voted 444 in favour, with only 94 of the Socialists voting against. The Reichstag members had voted to let Hitler and the Nazis do what they wanted. Germany had ceased to be a democracy.

F The main political parties and seats won

Main political parties	Seats won
Nazi Party	288
Nationalists (right wing)	52
Centre Party	74
Social Democrats (socialists, left wing)	120
Communists	81

Tasks

2   The cartoon (Source **E**) was published in the London *Evening Standard* on the 1 March 1933. This was the period after the passing of the Emergency Decree (see page 98). The election in Germany happened on 6 March 1933, with the results shown in Source **F**. What does this tell you about the cartoon and the cartoonist?

3   The Enabling Act was passed in March 1933. Using the information on pages 98–101, explain the reasons why this was possible.

■ The elimination of political opposition, 1933–34

Hitler acted swiftly to get rid of all political opposition to the Nazi Party. His biggest threat, the Communist Party, had been banned after the Reichstag Fire. Between May and July, all the other parties were banned, including those that had helped him to become Chancellor. Using his powers following the Enabling Act, Hitler passed a law against the formation of parties. This meant that the Nazi Party was the only political organisation allowed in Germany. Many prominent Socialists and Communists were arrested.

> 66 *The German Government has enacted the following law, which is herewith announced:*
>
> *Article I: The National Socialist German Workers' Party constitutes the only political Party in Germany.*
>
> *Article II: Whoever undertakes to maintain the organisational structure of another political Party or to form a new political Party will be punished with hard labour up to three years or with imprisonment up to three years, if the action is not subject to a greater penalty according to other regulations.* 99
>
> *The Reich Chancellor, Adolf Hitler*

G *The law against the formation of parties*

Trade unions, which had contained many communist supporters, were closed down in May 1933 and were replaced by the Nazis' own trade union, the German Labour Front.

In July 1933, Hitler also signed an agreement with the Pope, known as the *Concordat*. Catholics agreed to accept Hitler's promise that he would not interfere with Catholicism in Germany. This agreement with the Pope gave Hitler international prestige.

Hitler's elimination of the SA

By the summer of 1933, Hitler's dictatorship was nearly complete. However, he was not fully in control of the SA (the Brownshirts), who were under the leadership of Ernst Röhm. The SA had a reputation for violence and causing chaos, which continued to give the Nazis a bad name. Hitler wanted a professional army, not a rabble. Röhm had ambitions for the SA to become more powerful (there were about 2 million members) and Hitler saw that the SA could challenge his leadership. Röhm was also personally ambitious and a potential threat to Hitler.

Hitler had the SS (the Blackshirts) and he wanted them to replace the SA. He was told that Röhm and other SA leaders were plotting against him and planning to seize power immediately. (The first half of this statement has some truth in it; the second part does not!) Hitler decided to act.

Did you know ??????

The SS (the Blackshirts) were Hitler's personal bodyguards and loyal first and foremost to him.

> 66 *Adolf is a swine. He is betraying all of us. He is getting matey with the old generals who are a lot of old fogeys. Adolf knows what I want. I'm the nucleus of the new army.* 99
>
> *As recorded by an eyewitness who later left the Nazi Party and fled to England*

H *Röhm, leader of the SA, criticising Hitler during a drunken conversation*

Task

4 How reliable is Source **H** as evidence for Röhm's attitude towards Hitler in early 1934? Use Source **H** and your own knowledge to explain your answer.

On the night of 30 June 1934, Hitler used the SS to arrest and shoot leading members of the SA. The leading SA members had been having a meeting in a village inn near Munich. Just before 7am a number of SS cars careered into the village. Hitler was in one of them. He leapt out, marched inside and woke up Röhm with the words, 'You're under arrest.' The same process was repeated in other bedrooms. By 10am the SS began to round up other leading SA members in Berlin. Some were shot as they answered the door. Röhm himself was shot in his prison cell after he refused to commit suicide. The process continued for the next few days and nights.

Not all of those shot – in total about 200 – were SA members. The opportunity was taken to get rid of some other opponents in the process – for example, the previous Chancellor, von Schleicher.

Hitler told the Reichstag that he had acted swiftly to save the nation from a potential civil war. The Reichstag, consisting of only Nazis, accepted this version of events without question.

> 66 *A short meeting, and then Hitler's mind was made up. He decided not to wait until the morning but to hunt down the conspirators who were led by Röhm and the SA, and destroy the plot immediately. We arrived at 7.00am. We were able to enter the house and surprised a band of conspirators who were asleep. We took them prisoners at once. With great courage, Hitler personally made the arrests.* 99
>
> *From a radio broadcast by Goebbels, 1 July 1934*

I *An account of the Night of the Long Knives*

> ❝ The smoothness with which the murders of 30 June were carried out is powerful proof that no Röhm plot was imminent. There was no resistance encountered anywhere. Many victims unsuspectingly surrendered voluntarily, believing it was all a big mistake. The only shots fired were those of the executioners. ❞

Taken from Brachar, K. (1971) The German Dictatorship

J *A view of the Night of the Long Knives*

Task

5   How useful are Sources **I**, **J** and **K** for learning about the Night of the Long Knives? Use the sources and your own knowledge to explain your answer.

Key profile

Josef Goebbels

As a child, Goebbels (1897–1945) suffered from polio that left him with a club foot. This deformity had stopped him from fighting in the First World War. He joined the Nazi Party in 1922, and was quickly active in producing propaganda. In 1933, he was appointed Minister of Propaganda and Enlightenment, with control over all branches of the media and the arts. He was a brilliant speaker and fanatically loyal to Hitler.

THEY SALUTE WITH BOTH HANDS NOW.

K *The Night of the Long Knives: a cartoon by David Low. This cartoon appeared in a London newspaper on 3 July 1934. The person holding the spear is Göring. Goebbels is peeping between his master's legs*

The Führer

On 2 August 1934, President Hindenburg died. Hitler combined the offices of President and Chancellor, and became the Führer, or leader. The German armies swore a personal oath of loyalty to Hitler. He had gained total power within Germany.

One-party State

Hitler was all-powerful; he was the Führer. However, he was also personally lazy. He usually got up late and was very reluctant to read through routine paperwork. Much of the detailed work and decision making was left to others. He preferred to dream up grand schemes about the greatness of Nazi rule and his plans for the expansion of the German State. Hitler's chief subordinates were allowed a great deal of flexibility, but they knew what Hitler wanted.

Law and order

The Nazis abolished the right to trial before imprisonment. The justice system became part of the Nazi State. Judges were replaced where necessary by Nazi supporters. The SS and the Gestapo could put people in **concentration camps** without a trial. In 1934, Hitler set up the People's Court, which tried people for 'crimes against the State'. Any opponent of the Nazis was called an enemy of the State.

The SS and Gestapo

The SS had been formed in 1925 as Hitler's personal bodyguard. By the early 1930s, it had become the party's own police force. After the Night of the Long Knives in June 1934, it became the most important military group within the State under its leader, Heinrich Himmler.

The Gestapo was the secret police, first in the state of Prussia, then over the whole of Germany from 1936. Reinhard Heydrich became its head. Its job was to search out opponents of the Nazis, and it had the powers to arrest and imprison. It used informers to uncover any attempts to organise opposition. It used torture to extract information and confessions.

Concentration camps

Anyone arrested by the Gestapo could be held in 'protective custody' in a concentration camp indefinitely. When the camps were first established, there were over 100,000 prisoners. Most of them were political opponents. Once the Nazis had consolidated their power over the German people, there were fewer political prisoners.

The camps were run by SS guards – Death's Head Units – trained to be ruthless and cruel. Beatings were given for minor offences; anything more major resulted in execution without trial.

Key profile

Heinrich Himmler

Himmler (1900–45) had been a chicken farmer and was an early supporter of the Nazi Party. His loyalty to Hitler was rewarded in 1929 when he became head of Hitler's personal bodyguard, the SS. The organisation was ruthless in dealing with potential opposition to Hitler, as seen in the Night of the Long Knives. Later, the SS was responsible for much of the organisation for setting up death camps to exterminate the Jews.

L *Heinrich Himmler*

Propaganda

The Nazi State used propaganda ruthlessly to impose its own ideas over others. Josef Goebbels understood that propaganda worked best if the German people were given simple ideas with short slogans and powerful visual images. Therefore, criticising the Treaty of Versailles, making Germany great and blaming the Jews for Germany's disasters, could be presented in posters, newspapers, films, speeches and on radio.

Huge marches and rallies were organised to show the power and the achievements of Nazi Germany. Every September, from 1933 to 1938, a huge rally was held at Nuremberg. The event lasted several days and was a mixture of spectacle, parade, festival and religious ceremony. The film-maker Leni Riefenstahl was paid to produce films that glorified the Nazis using an event such as this, and they were shown at cinemas across Germany.

The largest propaganda event was when Berlin staged the Olympic Games in 1936. Everything was carefully stage managed. The stadium was, at the time, the largest in the world. News reports were carefully controlled, as was the filming of the event. During the games, the Nazi State was on show. Anti-Jewish slogans were removed from the streets of Berlin, and thousands of visitors went away with a very positive view of Nazi Germany.

Propaganda was used to promote Hitler as a powerful, yet caring, leader. Hitler was photographed with children or dogs and presented as a friendly person. He was also shown in photographs and posters as a military leader who had all the skills needed to lead Germany.

Many women adored him, and he received many flattering letters. Both men and women found much to admire in his achievements and were attracted to his promises.

> **Did you know** ? ? ? ? ? ?
>
> All filming of the Olympic Games was supervised by Leni Riefenstahl and she had to approve all camera crews. Her own film, *Olympia*, was the only official record of the games permitted and it was distributed worldwide.

> **Did you know** ? ? ? ? ? ?
>
> Hitler organised the games to show off the superiority of the German Aryan race. However, the American Black athlete, Jesse Owens, won four gold medals. Hitler refused to shake hands with Owens or to award his medals.

M *Hitler and the Nazi salute. This was a famous poster advertising the film* Triumph of the Will *by Leni Riefenstahl, 1935*

Censorship

Censorship influenced every aspect of daily life under the Nazis. The Nazis controlled what was heard, read or seen; nothing was allowed to contradict the propaganda concerning the greatness of the Nazi State.

The media

- German radio was brought under State control in 1934. All broadcasts were vetted by the propaganda ministry. Goebbels arranged for 6,000 loudspeakers to be set up in public places so that everyone could hear government announcements. Cheap radios were manufactured so that most families could afford to buy one. Foreign stations were difficult to tune in because of the wavebands used by the German stations.

- The only source of news allowed was the State-controlled press agency. Detailed instructions were given at daily press conferences about how the news was to be presented. The only newspapers allowed were Nazi-run.

- The cinema provided a similar mixture of entertainment and politics as that on the radio. Most popular were the escapist romances or adventures, which Hitler himself enjoyed watching. Only the work of Leni Riefenstahl was recognised as outstanding. Her most famous film was *Triumph of the Will,* a film about the 1934 party rally.

- Books not approved of by the Nazis were burnt. A huge bonfire organised by young Nazis in May 1933 resulted in 20,000 books being destroyed. Eventually, the works of over 2,500 writers were officially banned.

N *The burning of books in Berlin, May 1933*

Control of education

Education was controlled from the moment children started school, so that they learnt Nazi beliefs. In history, children were taught the Nazi version of the past, for example that Germany had been 'stabbed in the back' at the end of the First World War by German politicians who were influenced by the Jews.

Boys were taught military skills. Girls were taught housekeeping, cookery and how to be good mothers. For the older children, a new subject was introduced, Eugenics, that is the study of how to 'improve' the German race through selective breeding. All Jewish teachers were sacked. Other teachers had to take an oath of loyalty to Hitler.

Youth movements

Hitler also wanted to control young Germans out of school. He initiated youth organisations, which became compulsory to join after 1936. There were different groups for 6–10, 10–14 and 14–18 year olds. All groups were taught about Nazi beliefs, and given lots of physical exercise and training. The older boys were expected to learn military discipline, while for the girls there was the League of German Girls that aimed to make girls fit to become strong German mothers.

Many children and their families welcomed the youth movements. They provided opportunities for weekends away camping and hiking. In spite of the Nazi's view of women, girls could partially break free of the role of homemaker by travelling away and meeting teenagers from other areas of Germany.

Did you know ??????

In German schools, different subjects taught German propaganda. Biology taught that Aryan Germans were superior to all other races. Geography taught about the lands that had once been part of Germany and the need for more living space for Germans.

Did you know ??????

The Hitler Youth's emblem bore the swastika symbol, and its motto was 'Blood and Honour'. It was officially part of the SA, the Nazi Party's paramilitary group.

Ⓞ *Hitler Youth Rally in the 1930s*

❝ *Service in the Hitler Youth, we were told, was an honourable service to the German people. I was, however, not thinking of the Führer, nor of serving the German people, when I raised my right hand, but of the attractive prospect of participating in games, sports, hiking, singing, camping and other exciting activities away from school and the Home. A uniform, a badge, an oath, a salute. There seemed to be nothing to it.* ❞

Taken from M. MacKinnon The Naked Years: Growing up in Nazi Germany

Ⓟ *The memoirs of a member of the League of German Girls*

The increase in military exenditure stimulated other industries and provided many more jobs. Between 1933 and 1939, coal and chemical production doubled; oil, iron and steel trebled; and iron-ore mining increased 500 per cent.

Of course, the huge fall in unemployment from 6 million to virtually zero comes from the official Nazis figures. Some groups were not included, such as Jews dismissed from their jobs, and when all Jews lost the right to be German citizens none of them were counted. Neither were women who left employment with State financial offers to get married and raise a family. Opponents of the Nazis held in concentration camps did not count either.

Hitler's aim was to make Germany self-sufficient, because the country could not afford to pay for huge quantities of imports of raw materials. He didn't totally succeed. German heavy industry still remained dependent on Swedish iron ore and some food was still being imported. However, under the Four Year Plan, started in 1936, Germany was moving towards self-sufficiency.

Hitler wanted to achieve this goal by 1940 so that the German economy was ready for war.

E	Unemployment in Nazi Germany	
Year	Number	Total workforce
1933	6,014,000	25.9
1934	3,773,000	13.5
1935	2,974,000	10.3
1936	2,520,000	7.4
1937	1,853,000	4.1
1938	1,052,000	1.9
1939	302,000	0.5

Task

1. What conclusions can you reach from the statistics shown in Sources **A**, **C**, **D** and **E**?

> 66 *Apart from Germany and Italy, only Japan can be considered as a power standing firm in the face of the world peril posed by Communism. A victory of Communism over Germany would lead to the annihilation of the German people. If we do not succeed in bringing the German army as rapidly as possible to the rank of premier army in the world, then Germany will be lost. Now, with iron determination, a 100 per cent self-sufficiency should be achieved in every sphere where it is possible. I thus set the following tasks:*
>
> *1 The German armed forces must be operational within four years.*
>
> *2 The German economy must be fit for war within four years.* 99

Taken from Boxer, A. (2003) Germany 1918-1945

F Hitler's economic memorandum, 1936

Much was achieved. However, it would have been impossible for Germany to reach total self-sufficiency. There was not the necessary quantity of raw materials within the country's existing boundaries. It became clear to Hitler that the only solution would be for Germany to take over countries with the raw materials and food it needed. Hence, the Nazi policy of Lebensraum (living space) became closely linked with both economic policy and foreign policy.

Social policies and standards of living

Many Germans believed that Nazi rule was improving people's lives; unemployment had drastically reduced and few people were starving. Many people appreciated that actions were being taken to improve their economic situation. Even with wages improved a little, people tended not to dwell on the increased length of the average working week.

Small businesses often did well – especially where they had been competing with Jewish businesses that were closed down by the Nazis.

Big businesses benefited from the huge construction projects and big profits were made – so long as businesses were happy to produce what the Nazis wanted.

From July 1935, it became compulsory for all German men between the ages of 18 and 25 to do six months' work on practical projects. They were not paid wages, just pocket money, which was never very popular but did provide a sense of purpose for the unemployed.

The 'Strength Through Joy' organisation was part of the German Labour Front. It attempted to provide activities for leisure time to ensure a happy workforce. Holidays and cruises were the ones that attracted much publicity, but there were also concerts, theatre visits, sporting events and weekend trips provided at low cost. This gave ordinary workers access to activities previously enjoyed only by those better off.

As part of the 'Strength Through Joy' movement, Hitler wanted more Germans to have their own cars. The Volkswagen ('people's car') was designed and, in 1938, Hitler laid the foundation stone for the factory in which the cars would be built.

During the mid-1930s, many Germans were pleased with the effects of Nazi policies. Unemployment was falling and pride in Germany was rising, especially after they hosted the Olympic Games in Berlin in 1936. When Hitler successfully put troops in the demilitarised area of the Rhineland in the same year, Germans felt more secure from attack. Pride increased dramatically when Germany and Austria joined together in the *Anschluss* (union) of March 1938.

> ### Did you know ??????
> The average salary of managers rose by 70 per cent between 1934 and 1938.

> ### Did you know ??????
> Large numbers of German workers were persuaded to begin paying for a car on hire purchase even before production had begun. By the time war broke out in September 1939, no cars had been delivered and the factory was converted to producing military vehicles. No money paid in advance by the workers was refunded.

> ### Task
>
> **2** Using the information on these two pages, make two lists:
>
> a The ways in which Germans benefited socially.
>
> b The ways in which they didn't.

G *A poster from 1938 promoting the Volkswagen. It tells people to save five marks per week to buy their own car*

H *German workers on a trip organised by the 'Strength Through Joy' movement. The text on the bus reads 'Strength through Joy'*

Effects of Nazi policies on the lives of women

The Nazis preferred women to stick to what was seen as their 'natural' occupations of being wives and mothers. Nazi attitudes towards women were summed up by 'Kinder, Kirche und Küche' (Children, Church and Kitchen). Propaganda posters and paintings showed the ideal Nazi family.

Task

3 How useful is Source I for learning about life in Nazi Germany? Use Source I and your own knowledge to explain your answer.

I *Propaganda painting showing the ideal Nazi family. This was painted by Wolfgang Willrich in the 1930s*

The Nazis were worried about what had been a falling birth rate and wanted to promote the 'racially-pure' Aryan race. Therefore, incentives were introduced to encourage women to have children. For example, the Law for the Reduction of Unemployment in June 1933 introduced interest-free loans of up to 1,000 Reichmarks for young married couples on condition that the wife gave up work. A quarter of the loan was cancelled each time a child was born. The most productive mothers were awarded special medals at a ceremony held every year on the birthday of Hitler's mother. Laws against abortion were strictly enforced. From 1936, the Nazis opened special maternity homes designed to be breeding centres for the production of pure Aryan children. Racially-approved Aryan mothers were matched with SS men with the intention of filling Hitler's Germany with pure-bred German children.

German women who held positions of responsibility were sacked from their jobs. This happened to thousands of women doctors and civil servants in 1933. The number of women teachers was gradually reduced. From 1936, women could no longer be judges or serve on juries.

There were even campaigns to affect the way women dressed and looked. Hair should be worn in plaits or a bun; not dyed or permed. Make-up was discouraged, as were trousers. Slimming was criticised as women had to be capable of healthy child-bearing.

However, Nazi policies towards women were not always as successful as they seemed. For example, the priority given to rearmament meant that there was a shortage of building materials for houses. This meant that young couples wishing to have a large family found it difficult to find or afford a suitable house. Also, when a shortage of workers was apparent in the later 1930s, many more women did paid work. By 1939, many more women were in paid employment compared with 1933. In 1937, the Nazis were forced to change a clause in their marriage loans scheme. Now married women who had a loan could, after all, take up a paid job.

Effects of Nazi policies on German culture

German culture was restricted through censorship and propaganda. For example, modern art was dismissed as 'degenerate'. Plays and films were checked for having suitable themes that promoted Nazi ideals. The tolerant permissive society of Weimar Germany with its nightclubs and American music was banned. So was the work of Jewish writers and composers. Overall, new developments in the arts were stifled. Instead, Nazi propaganda pervaded everything.

Many artists and authors suffered in silence. However, some chose to emigrate – as did scientists. The most famous one was Albert Einstein, who later helped to develop the nuclear bomb in the USA during the Second World War.

To begin with, in 1933, the benefits of Nazi rule appeared to outweigh the disadvantages and concerns that many people had; living standards appeared to be recovering from the Depression, pride in Germany was certainly increasing, and many workers who had supported the Communists were benefiting from Nazi rule so long as they were obedient. The negatives – political, social and cultural – only became prominent in many people's minds in the later 1930s, when the Nazis had achieved totalitarian control.

> **Did you know** ??????
>
> German playwright Bertolt Brecht was forced to flee his country in 1933. His plays portrayed German society in a negative light and were critical of Nazism.

Task

4   Do you think that the German people benefited from the Nazi rule in 1933–39?

You will need to consider:

- the ways in which Germans did benefit and ways in which they did not
- which Germans benefited
- whether there was a change in the balance between 'benefiting' and 'not benefiting' in the period 1933–39.

> **AQA** *Examiner's tip*
>
> To answer this question, draw up lists, positive and negative for political, social and cultural aspects. Then write a detailed explanation that reaches a judgement.

Racial persecution: the Jews and other alien groups

The Nazis believed that the Jews were members of an inferior race. True Germans, by contrast, were the master race destined to rule over other races. The worst of the inferior races was the Jews, and therefore it was the duty of the Nazi State to persecute them.

Even before he had come to power, Hitler had made clear his racial views in detail. These had appeared in *Mein Kampf*, as well as in many speeches and in pamphlets and posters produced by the Nazis. The Jews were accused of being, not just inferior, but also of joining with the Communists to cause Germany's defeat in the First World War. Jews had, Hitler claimed, continued to undermine Germany after 1918.

When Hitler came to power in 1933, there were only half a million Jews in Germany, less than one per cent of the total population. However, many of them did have important positions in society in businesses and in professions. Especially in some cities, many doctors, lawyers and bankers were Jews. This gave the impression that it was the Jews who were controlling society and the economy. When Hitler took over Austria in March 1938, there was a large concentration of Jews in the capital, Vienna, and this reinforced Hitler's views about how much the Jews were in control.

Hitler had no organised policy to begin with, but some extremists in the Nazi Party encouraged actions against the Jews.

- April 1933 – Official one-day boycott of Jewish shops, lawyers and doctors throughout Germany. After this, members of the SA stood outside shops and physically prevented customers from entering.
- 1934 – Anti-Jewish propaganda increased.
- September 1935 – The Nuremberg Laws provided legal restrictions on Jews:
  1 The Law for the Protection of German Blood and Honour banned marriages between Jews and Aryans, and banned sexual relations outside marriage.
  2 The Reich Citizenship Law made Jews 'subjects' rather than 'citizens', and this meant that Jews lost some legal rights.
- 1936 – There was a lull in the persecution of the Jews during the Berlin Olympic Games. Anti-Jewish slogans were removed from the streets and from Jewish shops and businesses.
- September 1937 – Hitler spoke out against the Jews, and many Jewish businesses were seized by the Nazis.
- June–July 1938 – Jewish doctors, dentists and lawyers were forbidden to treat Aryans.
- October 1938 – Jews had to have a red letter 'J' stamped on their passports.
- November 1938 – *Kristallnacht*.

Key terms

Kristallnacht: (the Night of Broken Glass) the Nazis coordinated an attack on Jewish people and their property on the night of 9 November 1938.

Kristallnacht (the Night of Broken Glass) happened after a Jewish youth shot and killed a German embassy official in Paris. Josef Goebbels, the propaganda minister, announced that there should be 'demonstrations' against the Jews during the night of 9 November. The violence that this encouraged led to the attacking of 8,000 Jewish shops and homes and most of the Jewish synagogues in Germany. About 100 Jews were killed and over 20,000 arrested and sent to concentration camps.

> 66 *Jewish buildings were smashed into and contents demolished or looted. It was all carried out by SS men armed with hammers, axes, crowbars and incendiary bombs. Three synagogues were set on fire. Jewish males aged between 16 and 60 were arrested and transported to concentration camps. All of the local crowds observing were shocked by the fury of these Nazi actions.* 99
>
> An account of Kristallnacht in Leipzig, by the man in charge of the American embassy in that city

J *Kristallnacht in Leipzig*

Much of the property damaged on Kristallnacht was rented by Jews from German owners. The Nazis took the opportunity to fine the Jews 1 billion Reichsmarks to repair the damage. Any remaining Jewish businesses were confiscated, and Jewish pupils were only allowed to attend Jewish schools. Jews were expected to do the worst jobs and German people were encouraged to treat Jews badly. This was even more so after Hitler had taken over Austria in March 1938 and the same policies were followed there.

Did you know ??????
The youth who shot the German official in Paris was Herschel Grynszpan. He did so because he had received a letter from his family explaining that they were among 8,000 Jews expelled from Germany waiting in harsh conditions at the border for entry to Poland.

Did you know ??????
Attacks on Jews such as the Kristallnacht are known as pogroms. They became increasingly common from 1938 onwards in Germany and other countries such as Austria. They were often encouraged by the Nazi Party, but sometimes occurred spontaneously.

Did you know ??????
Kristallnacht sparked international outrage. It discredited pro-Nazi movements in Europe and North America, leading to the eventual decline of their support.

K *Jews cleaning the streets of Vienna, 1938. Notice the expressions on the faces of on-lookers*

In 1939, Jews were officially encouraged to emigrate. Not all could afford to do so – or get visas. The first mass arrests of Jews took place in March 1939. Nearly 30,000 Jewish men and boys were sent to concentration camps.

Task

5 Compare the treatment of Jews in the 1930s by summarising the position of Jews at the end of:

a 1933

b 1935

c 1938.

6 What do you think were the three most important turning-points for Jews in Germany between 1933 and 1939? Explain your answer.

The treatment of undesirable groups

The Nazis also acted against other groups seen as being alien. Gypsies had been unpopular for a long time because they did not have regular jobs and they moved around. Many Germans were happy when the Nuremberg Laws of 1935 were applied to gypsies. They were increasingly persecuted in the later 1930s. Similarly, tramps and beggars were arrested and put to forced labour.

Those with physical disabilities or mental problems were seen as a threat to Aryan superiority if they were allowed to have children. Therefore, a law, passed as early as July 1933, included compulsory sterilisation. This included people with depression, epilepsy, blindness, deafness and the physically disabled. By 1937, almost 200,000 compulsory sterilisations had been performed on men and women. Later policies included euthanasia, or 'mercy killing', by means of lethal injection.

The mistreatment of Jews and other 'undesirable' groups got worse very quickly after the war started in September 1939.

Did you know ??????

Because gypsies have a tradition of oral history rather than written history, less is known about their experiences of the Nuremberg Laws than about any other group that was subjected to them.

Activity

1 Draw up a table in two columns to compare what life was like for different groups of people living in Germany at the beginning of 1933 and the beginning of 1939.

AQA Examination-style questions

5 Study **Source A** and then answer **both** parts of the question that follows.
   In your answers, you should refer to the source by its letter.

Source A Scene from a Hitler Youth Camp

(a) Using **Source A** and your own knowledge, describe how Hitler and the
     Nazis influenced the minds of young Germans through education and youth
     activities.   *(8 marks)*

(b) 'Hitler was able to become Chancellor of Germany in January 1933 mainly
     because of the effects of the Wall Street Crash.'
     Do you agree? Explain your answer.   *(12 marks)*

6 Depression and the New Deal: the USA, 1929–41

6.1 How serious were the effects of the Depression on the American people?

A *Franklin D. Roosevelt*

Objectives

In this chapter you will learn about:

how serious the effects of the Depression were on the American people

how Roosevelt dealt with the Depression

how far the New Deal was successful in ending the Depression in the USA.

In the 1920s, many Americans had prospered during the '**boom**' years; confidence in the stock market was high and share prices had continued to rise. Then, in 1929, prices fell; confidence was destroyed; many businesses and banks became bankrupt, and millions lost their jobs. By 1932, nearly one-quarter of the workforce was unemployed. President Hoover had failed to end the growing Depression.

In 1933, the new President, Franklin D. Roosevelt, took office and promised the American people a New Deal. Many measures were introduced, with the State providing jobs for millions. The economy improved to some extent, but it was very dependent on government money. Indeed, the Government took over many responsibilities for people's welfare, and this went against the American tradition of individuals looking after themselves. Some people objected, and the highest court in America, the US Supreme Court, declared some parts of the New Deal unlawful because they went against the US constitution.

Only when the Second World War had started and produced the need for huge volumes of American exports was the American economy able to fully recover.

Key terms

Boom: a period of rapid economic growth with rising output, employment and profits – opposite of a slump.

∞ links

For more information on the 1920s Boom, see Chapter 3 pages 58–62.

The effects of the Wall Street Crash

The Wall Street Stock Exchange in New York crashed on 24 October 1929. The day became known as 'Black Thursday' when over 1.3 million shares were sold. As prices tumbled, panic selling occurred. The crash had been foreshadowed during the previous week when some investors had sold their shares. After the initial crash, big banks tried to restore confidence by buying up great numbers of shares, but this only worked for a short time and prices began to fall again. Prices continued to fall for three years until shares on average had lost 80 per cent of their value.

Over 100,000 companies went bankrupt during the period 1929–33 and were forced to close. Others survived by reducing their workforce and their production levels. By 1933, the production of manufactured goods was less than one-fifth of the level it was before the crash.

Banks suffered badly because many had invested their customers' money in shares that rapidly lost value. Banks tried to recover money by demanding the repayment of loans from companies, but this meant that even more businesses were forced to close, leading to even more unemployment.

These events led to a period of huge economic depression – first of all in the USA, and then around the world.

B *Scene outside the New York Stock Exchange on Wall Street after the crash in October 1929*

> **Did you know** ??????
>
> 'Black Thursday' was followed by 'Black Monday' and 'Black Tuesday' as the crash got worse.

Timeline

America, 1929–41

1929	The Wall Street Crash started the Great Depression.
1932	12 million were unemployed in the USA. Franklin D. Roosevelt was elected as President to replace Hoover.
1933	The New Deal began.
1936	Problems in the Supreme Court over some of the New Deal. Roosevelt elected for second term of office.
1939	Second World War began in Europe, with the USA isolationist.
1940	The USA involvement in Lend-Lease programme.
1941 Dec	Japan bombed Pearl Harbour. The USA declared war on Japan and then Germany.

∞ links

For the background to the Wall Street Crash and details on what happened, see pages 72–73.

Task

1   What can you learn by studying Source **B**?

Unemployment and its effects

Unemployment rose rapidly so that, by 1932, it affected about one-quarter of the workforce – 12 million people. Those in work often suffered pay cuts as businesses tried to keep going and, as a consequence they suffered a drop in their standard of living.

Every group in American society was affected by the Depression – economically, but also psychologically. Even professional people were affected; they had invested in shares or in bank accounts and in either case they often lost most of their money. There were fewer opportunities for managerial positions as businesses went bankrupt. Many lost confidence in themselves and in the USA, with its proud record of economic expansion over the previous decades. Many Americans blamed the greed of business leaders.

In cities and towns, wage earners suffered a drop in income from 1929 to 1932. Weekly earnings in manufacturing for those lucky enough to keep a job during these years dropped from $28 a week to $22. It continued to fall in 1933. Unemployment in the cities was not spread evenly among the workforce. It was particularly high among workers in heavy industries and among blacks.

Many in the cities tried to find jobs such as selling newspapers or apples on street corners, or setting up as shoeshine boys. Others simply begged.

Task

2 What can you learn about the effects of the Depression by studying Source **C**?

C Street sellers on 42nd Street near Broadway, New York, 1932

Struggling farmers

D *An impoverished family on a New Mexico highway. They had moved as refugees from Iowa in 1932*

Did you know ??????

During this period of agricultural depression, farmers suffered from the 'dust bowl' – severe dust storms, caused by drought and over-farming.

Farmers were also very badly hit. By 1933, farm incomes had dropped by about 60 per cent compared with 1929. Meanwhile, the goods that farmers needed to buy, such as industrial products, dropped in price by only 15 per cent. Therefore, farmers could only afford to buy about half of what they could afford before 1929.

Many farmers had to sell up because they could not afford to repay loans to banks. Even wealthy farmers in once-prosperous regions such as Iowa were badly affected. In the Midwest, farmers suffered an extra blow. Over-farming had led to the soil becoming infertile. In the early 1930s, there were droughts and strong winds that blew away the fertile topsoil.

Many tenant farmers were forced off the land as farmers no longer needed them – or could not afford to keep them. Many moved on to the roads and travelled around looking for work. Many tried to travel illegally in the boxcars of American railroads. By 1933, the USA had about a million people travelling around. Most of them were drifting aimlessly. Many of them had had good records as workers. Now they were feeling helpless despite not being to blame for their situation.

Suffering was particularly bad for the children of the unemployed. Many lacked proper clothing or an adequate diet.

Many homeless unemployed people constructed their own homes in shanty towns on the edge of towns or in cities. As President Hoover was blamed for their plight, the shanty towns became known as Hoovervilles.

Did you know ??????

John Steinbeck's famous novels *The Grapes of Wrath* and *Of Mice and Men* depict the lives of former tenant farmers forced to travel to search for work as a result of the Depression.

Activity

1   Read part (or all) of a novel such as *The Grapes of Wrath* by John Steinbeck to investigate how the Depression affected the lives of millions of Americans. Alternatively, watch the famous 1940 film based on this book.

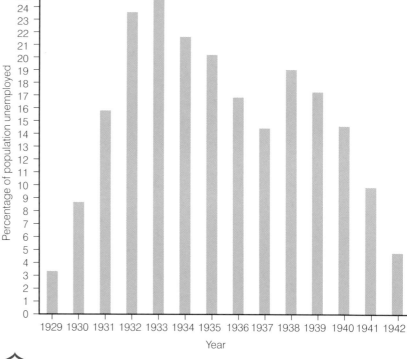

The attempts of Hoover's government to deal with the Depression

Hoover had become President in early 1929 at the height of the boom of the 1920s. He had great confidence in the business system of the USA and believed that the government should interfere as little as possible. When faced with the crisis in late-1929, he believed that voluntary cooperation between government and business would solve the problems. He held conferences with business leaders to get agreements that they would maintain production and employment levels. He did offer over $4,000 million for major building projects in the construction industries to provide new jobs. For example, work started in 1931 on the building of the Hoover Dam on the Colorado river. He cut taxes so that people had more money to spend.

E Unemployment in the USA, 1929–42

The government tried to help farmers by buying up food at above-market prices, but this encouraged farmers to grow more, rather than encouraging them to produce less. The Hawley-Smoot Tariff of 1930 was the highest in American history, with average duties of 40 per cent on both agricultural and industrial goods, and it was intended to discourage imports. However, other countries retaliated, and even less was exported from the USA. Farmers were left with their huge surpluses.

In 1930, with mounting unemployment, Hoover tried to coordinate the work of voluntary agencies. He insisted that helping the poor was mainly the role of local communities and local government. However, by late-1931, many cities were nearly bankrupt from the relief programmes they had been operating to provide food and shelter. In 1932, Hoover was forced to approve the Emergency Relief Act which provided $300 million to states to help the unemployed.

By 1932, with unemployment at 12 million, Hoover set up the Reconstruction Finance Corporation (RFC), which provided loans of $1,500 million to businesses to help them recover from the Depression. Even this failed to have much impact.

Key profile

Herbert Hoover

Hoover (1874–1964), a successful mining engineer, became a millionaire by the age of 35. During the First World War, he played a major part in humanitarian relief in Europe. In 1920, he joined the Republican Party and became Secretary of State for Commerce. In 1928, he was elected President.

Tasks

3 List in bullet-point form the things Hoover did to try to end the Depression.

4 In pairs or small groups, discuss the reasons why the Depression continued in spite of Hoover's efforts.

F Herbert Hoover

The unpopularity of Hoover and the election of Roosevelt

Hoover

President Hoover was blamed for the Depression – mostly unfairly. He did, however, have great difficulty in appreciating the extent of the crisis and the scale of the help that was needed. He had been elected by the Republicans to continue the policy of as little government interference as possible – the policies of laissez-faire and rugged individualism.

Now in power, Hoover found it difficult to change his policies sufficiently to deal with the deepening crisis. His term of office was dominated by the Depression and he was blamed for not intervening directly on a large scale, even though he did more than any other previous president.

As explained, he did expand government lending and he did encourage public works schemes. However, he could not bring himself to consider more direct action. He could not abandon the principles of self-help and voluntary cooperation. He continued to believe that the economy had to right itself. He said: 'Economic depression cannot be cured by government action. Economic wounds must be healed by the producers and consumers themselves'.

Historians have recently been more sympathetic towards Hoover, seeing him as the victim of one of the worst crises in American history. However, only later in the 1930s did economists such as John Maynard Keynes argue that direct government action was necessary. Even if Hoover had wanted to do this, his Republican-controlled Congress would not have approved. Indeed, most members of Congress were pleased that Hoover was trying to balance the budget. People's belief in him was severely damaged by 1932 – and this was made worse by his actions over the war veterans.

After the First World War, the government was paying annual amounts to the war veterans – that is, those who had fought and suffered disabilities. In addition, it had been agreed that in 1945 they should be paid a 'bonus'. However, as the Depression hit many of them badly, they said they needed the bonus immediately. A march to Washington was organised and in June 1932 about 20,000 camped outside Washington. **The House of Representatives** voted in favour of immediate payment, but **the Senate** overruled it on grounds of cost. Hoover offered $100,000 for their transport home.

However, many refused to go home and some moved their squat close to the White House. Hoover feared the outbreak of violence. Hoover called in troops under General Douglas MacArthur, and he used tanks, infantry and tear gas to move the squatters and destroy their camps. Many marchers were injured and two babies died from the effects of the gas. It was a major political blunder by Hoover as he lost a lot of public sympathy.

> **Did you know** ??????
>
> Hoover's term of office was dominated by the Depression and he was blamed for not intervening directly on a large scale, even though he did so more than any other previous president. Historians have recently been more sympathetic towards him, seeing him as the victim of one of the worst crises in American history.

> ∞ **links**
>
> See page 61 for more information about 'laissez-faire' and 'rugged individualism'.

> **Key terms**
>
> **The House of Representatives and the Senate:** the two Houses of Congress. Both of the Houses of Congress and the President have to agree before a law can be passed.

Roosevelt

By contrast, in 1932, Franklin D. Roosevelt, the Democratic candidate for the presidency, was full of enthusiasm and charisma. As Governor of New York (1928–32), Roosevelt had a reputation for listening and then acting. He had already intervened to try to improve the economy in New York State. For example, he had increased income tax to provide an extra $20 million for emergency relief during the winter of 1931–32. Although this was seen as a temporary measure to meet a crisis, it was the first state-run relief effort in the USA.

Without going into specific details, Roosevelt created the impression that he would act. He used the radio effectively. He spoke of the need for government to help 'the forgotten man'. When he was accepted by the Democratic Party as its candidate, he stated boldly:

'I pledge you, I pledge myself, to a new deal for the American people. This is more than a political campaign. Give me your help, not to win votes alone, but to aim in this crusade to restore America to its people.'

As well as using the radio, Roosevelt made whistle-stop tours across America, promising action and giving hope to many Americans. He made it clear that he would use the government to act, but would also cooperate with big business.

The Presidential Election of November 1932 gave Roosevelt a large majority. He received 57 per cent of the popular vote; Hoover received 40 per cent. (In 1928, Hoover had received 58 per cent and the Democratic candidate 40 per cent.) More significantly, Roosevelt won in 42 out of the total 48 states in the USA. This shows that he had the majority support in most areas of the USA.

> *Hoover happened to be in a bad spot. The Depression came on, and there he was. If Jesus Christ had been there, he'd have had the same problem. It's too bad for poor old Hoover that he happened to be there. This was a worldwide Depression. It wasn't Hoover's fault. In 1932, a Chinaman or a monkey could have been elected against him, no question about it.*
>
> From an interview with a businessman in New York just after Hoover's defeat in 1932

G Hoover's problems as President

Key profile

Franklin D. Roosevelt

Roosevelt (1882–1945) was born into a wealthy family, trained as a lawyer, but went into politics. In 1921, he suffered from polio – often a fatal disease at that time. During his long recovery, he studied politics and, in 1928, became Governor of New York State. In 1932, he campaigned as the Democratic candidate for the presidency.

Did you know ??????

Roosevelt survived polio, but for the rest of his life he was only able to walk with leg braces. Although he had difficulty in getting around and often had to rely on colleagues to help him, the media never took advantage by showing pictures of him stumbling or looking like an invalid. He was always shown either sitting or standing in a situation where he could lean against something.

Task

5   Using Source **G** and your own knowledge, explain why Roosevelt was successful in defeating Hoover in the Presidential Election of 1932.

In order to answer the question, you need to consider:

▪ the reasons why Hoover was unpopular

▪ what Roosevelt did and said to make him a strong candidate

▪ what Source **G** is saying, and judge whether you think it is accurate. Looking at the election result details will help you to form a balanced view about Hoover's chances of success.

Did you know ??????

The US constitution, dating from 1787, laid down that the successful presidential candidate's term of office started in March following the November election. The constitution was amended in 1933 so that a new president now starts in January.

6.2 How did Roosevelt deal with the Depression?

Roosevelt was elected in November 1932, but did not take office until March 1933. Meanwhile, the economic situation in the USA was getting steadily worse. In fact, Roosevelt was lucky to start his presidency at all. Two weeks before he took office, an assassin fired five bullets at him at close range. Roosevelt was unharmed, but the Mayor of Chicago who was with Roosevelt was killed.

After he had become President, Roosevelt started a hectic period of reforms, known as 'The Hundred Days'. He was determined to act quickly, and the measures have collectively become known as the New Deal. However, it is wrong to think that everything Roosevelt's government did was part of a carefully-planned programme. It is better to see what happened as specific responses to particular crises. The one common thread running through all that Roosevelt did was that the role of the government was greatly increased.

> **Did you know** ??????
>
> Roosevelt's fireside chats were carefully crafted to appeal to the masses. Language was kept simple, and anecdotes were used to explain complex issues. The time of broadcast was chosen so that people in all American time zones would be able to listen.

Roosevelt's fireside chats

A Roosevelt preparing to start his first fireside chat to the American people, March 1933

Roosevelt was the first American president to appreciate how he could use the media. He talked freely to the press and gained the confidence of many newspaper editors. However, he is best remembered for his fireside chats, the first one of which was in March 1933. He sat in front of a fire in his office and spoke directly to the American people on the radio. His talks became very popular and were listened to by millions of Americans. His voice was reassuring and he helped people to believe that everything was going to be all right.

Over the radio, he invited people to write to him about their problems. Mail arrived by the truckload, and a staff of 50 was needed to handle all of his correspondence. By contrast, Hoover had employed one person for the same job.

> 66 *Some of our bankers have shown themselves either incompetent or dishonest in their handling of the people's funds. They had used money entrusted to them in speculations and unwise loans... [It was] the Government's job to straighten out this situation and do it as quickly as possible. And the job is being performed... Confidence and courage are the essentials of our plan... [We] must have faith; you must not be stampeded by rumours... We have provided the machinery to restore our financial system; it is up to you to support and make it work. Together we cannot fail.* 99

B *From Roosevelt's first 'Fireside Chat', 12 March 1933*

The New Deal

Roosevelt introduced what became known as the New Deal with a flurry of acts designed to restore confidence. He had said when he became President:

> 66 *The only thing we have to fear is fear itself – nameless, unreasoning, unjustified terror which paralyses needed efforts to convert retreat into advance... This nation calls for action and action now.* 99

Within the first 100 days, he started a wide range of programmes designed to deal with the banking crisis, restore confidence in the stock exchange, help agriculture and industry, and provide relief to the homeless and unemployed. All of this involved the government acting much more in important areas of life than American governments had done previously. The New Deal's programme became known as Relief, Recovery and Reform.

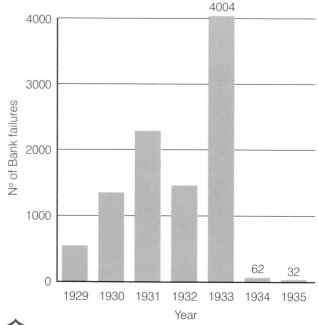

C *Bank failures, 1929–35*

Task

1 From what you have studied so far, what do you think Roosevelt meant by each of the three words:

■ Relief

■ Recovery

■ Reform?

The banking crisis

During the presidency of Hoover, many banks had gone bankrupt as businesses were unable to repay their loans. This had caused misery for millions of Americans who lost their savings in these banks.

By the time that Roosevelt became President, banks were closed in many states of the USA, and many investors were withdrawing their savings from those that had remained open. So Roosevelt closed all the banks throughout the USA for four days to give time for new laws to be passed.

The Emergency Banking Relief Act restored confidence in banking by giving the government strict control over banks. Only the sounder banks were allowed to reopen. The government guaranteed that all money put into the banks up to the value of $2,500 would be safe because it would be covered by the Federal Deposit Insurance Corporation.

At the same time, Roosevelt acted to restore confidence in the stock exchange with government agencies overseeing activities and preventing bad or risky practices. This helped people to resume trading.

Task

2 a Explain why the Banking Crisis of 1933 happened.

b Explain what President Roosevelt did to end it.

Farming: the Agricultural Adjustment Act, May 1933

In the 1920s, overproduction had been the biggest problem in agriculture. Unsold cotton in early 1933 in the USA was already more than the total average annual world consumption of American cotton. After ploughing up 10.5m acres of cotton, the price went up from 6.5 cents per pound to 10 cents per pound in 1933.

Falling incomes meant many farms were being handed over to banks in order to pay off debts. Roosevelt aimed to make farming more efficient by ending overproduction. This would be achieved by farming less land and finding jobs for displaced farm workers.

In May 1933, a new agency called the Agricultural Adjustment Administration (AAA) was set up. It paid farmers to reduce their production of main items, e.g. cotton. This would drive up prices.

There was, however, much more criticism of destroying food when millions of Americans were starving. There was public outcry when 6 million piglets were killed, even though many were later used to feed the unemployed. The government was helped by a drought in 1933, which made the wheat harvest the poorest since 1896. In the next few years, tobacco, beef and dairy farmers were brought into the scheme, encouraged to do so by the subsidies offered and by further droughts in the mid-west.

Overall, the work of the AAA led to better standards of living for farmers. Between 1932 and 1935 total farm income rose from $4.5 billion to $6.9 billion. The act was very popular with farmers. Ninety five per cent of tobacco growers signed up for AAA agreements. As an emergency measure, the AAA did deal effectively with the crisis of overproduction.

Relief: the Federal Emergency Relief Administration, May 1933

The Federal Emergency Relief Administration (FERA) was given $500 million to be divided equally among the states to help with the unemployed. Half the money went straight to the states; the other half was conditional on each state spending money on relief. Roosevelt chose Harry Hopkins to run this programme. He had administered the relief programmes that Roosevelt had introduced when Governor of New York.

However, many state governments refused to consider spending more, and considered that the poor were in that position through their own fault. Those needing relief were often treated badly in some states. Claimants were often kept waiting in long queues in hot weather. Even after filling in forms, there were long delays in making payments.

Although what was achieved under FERA was often disappointing, it did establish the idea of the **Federal government** giving funds directly for relief.

> **Did you know ??????**
>
> The Governor of Oregon went as far as to suggest euthanasia (mercy killing) for the needy and sick. The Governor of Georgia offered the unemployed a dose of castor oil.

> **Key terms**
>
> **Federal government:** the national government, based in Washington. Each of the 48 states had its own state government.

Relief: the Civil Works Administration, November 1933

The Civil Works Administration (CWA) was set up to provide emergency relief during the winter of 1933–34. It provided work on public projects for 4 million people during the winter before being closed down.

FERA agreed to follow this up with more funded public works projects itself.

Relief: the Civilian Conservation Corps, March 1933

Unemployed young men aged from 17 to 24 (later increased to 28) were recruited by the Department of Labour to work in the Civilian Conservation Corps (CCC) in national forests, parks and other public areas. It was originally set up for two years, but was extended throughout the 1930s. Altogether, about 3 million young people were involved.

They lived in camps, were provided with food and shelter, and received a small wage. They planted 1.3bn trees and contributed to all aspects of work in the countryside. For example, they dealt with forest fires, and installed 65,100 miles of telephone lines in remote areas. Many young men benefited from the experiences and training provided.

However, the CCC was criticised for focusing on mostly white men, and there was no guarantee of a job afterwards.

Welfare: the National Recovery Administration, June 1933

The National Recovery Administration (NRA) set out to improve working conditions in industry and outlawed child labour. It set out fair wages. Employees had the right to join a trade union.

Each industry was encouraged to adopt a code of practice that was fair to workers. Eventually, 557 codes were drawn up covering most industries. However, there were many criticisms of how they operated, and the Supreme Court later declared the NRA to be unlawful.

∞links

See page 133 for more information about criticism of the NRA.

Did you know ??????

Firms that adopted a code of fair practice were allowed to display a blue eagle with the logo, 'We do our part' printed underneath. Consumers were encouraged to support those firms that displayed the blue eagle.

D *A PWA work party doing dam construction*

Recovery: the Public Works Administration, June 1933

The Public Works Administration (PWA) was funded with $3.3 billion and its purpose was '**pump priming**'. That is, it was hoped that expenditure on public works such as roads, dams, hospitals and schools would stimulate the economy. For example, road building would lead to increased demand for concrete, which would encourage employment, and these workers would have more money to spend.

The work was carefully planned; the government did not want to be accused of wasting money on badly-thought out projects. The Secretary of the Interior, Harold Ickes, was in charge, and he demanded value for money. In any case, public works projects involve lengthy preparations with planning and organising contracts, and progress was bound to be slow. Eventually, the PWA was responsible for building 50,000 miles of roads and 13,000 schools. In the west, dams were built which helped to irrigate land that had been semi-desert, produce electricity and create four large National Parks. Hundreds of thousands of people gained jobs through these projects.

Recovery: the Works Progress Administration, 1935

Later, in a second wave of government activity, the Works Progress Administration (WPA) was set up and became a major employer. At any one time, it had about 2 million employees. Wages were reasonable, but lower than those in private industry.

The WPA was not allowed to compete for contracts with private firms or to build private houses. However, it did build 1,000 airport landing fields, 8,000 schools and hospitals, and 12,000 playgrounds. People were taken on for one year and given employment opportunities. In theory, the WPA took on jobs that private companies did not want. Many of its projects such as surveying historic sites would not have been carried out by private contractors.

> 66 *Give a man the dole and you save his body and destroy his spirit. Give him a job and pay him an assured wage and you save both the body and the spirit.* 99
>
> *The boss of the WPA, Harry Hopkins*

E *The value of the WPA*

> **Key terms**
>
> **Pump priming**: an expression used to suggest government spending would lead to economic growth.

> **Did you know** ??????
>
> Roosevelt appointed Ickes as his Secretary of the Interior in 1933. In the six years following his appointment, Ickes spent more than $5 billion through the PWA on various large-scale projects.

Task

3   a   Work out what Source **E** is saying about the purpose of the New Deal.

   b   Look back at each of the New Deal measures described so far. Did they all follow the same principle? Write a list of New Deal measures. Beside each, put a tick or a cross and write a reason to explain your answer.

Recovery: the Tennessee Valley Authority, May 1933

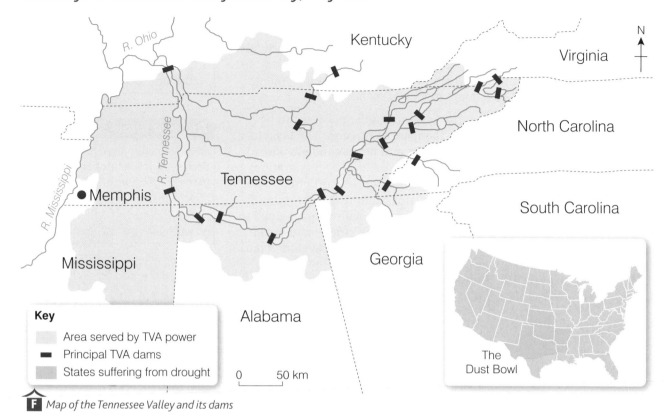

F *Map of the Tennessee Valley and its dams*

The Tennessee Valley Authority (TVA) was one of the biggest schemes of the New Deal. The river Tennessee ran through seven of the poorest states in the USA. The aim was to construct 20 dams to control the floods that affected the region from time to time. In dry seasons, much of the land was becoming a dust bowl. Farming could then develop more successfully, with more use of fertilisers. Another major aspect was the development of hydroelectric power in an area where few farms at the time had any electricity.

Relief: the Home Owners Loan Corporation, 1933

The Home Owners Loan Corporation (HOLC) gave out new loans to home buyers. Mortgage rates were low to try to prevent buyers from losing their homes. The intention was to stimulate the housing market. Three hundred thousand loans were given out within a year.

Relief: the Social Security Act, 1935

This was the first federal action providing old-age pensions for over 65s and unemployment insurance. However, it had to be self-financing, paid for by employees and employers. Pensions were not paid at a flat rate, but according to how much the worker had previously contributed, and they would not start until 1940. Unemployment benefits were low and paid for only a limited period – a maximum of $18 a week for 16 weeks.

However, this was a big step towards providing welfare for those in need, and it was criticised by many political opponents of Roosevelt.

Task

4 In what ways did the New Deal seek to provide help to American citizens?

Write an essay in response to this question. Firstly, think how it could be organised into 'themes' – that is, the types of help that the New Deal tried to provide. Then organise your answer so that each theme is dealt with in turn.

6.3   How far was the New Deal successful in ending the Depression in the USA?

The effectiveness and the limitations of the New Deal

Between 1933 and early 1935, Roosevelt had persuaded Congress to pass a lot of acts; unemployment was beginning to fall; and the economy seemed to be recovering.

Never had a government been so energetic in passing laws in peacetime. The US government had never taken so much responsibility for the running of the economy or for people's welfare.

However, Roosevelt was also facing a lot of criticism. The criticism came from those who thought his government was trying to do too much, as well as those who thought the opposite. Either way, all the activity generated by the New Deal appeared to be slowing down, so Roosevelt decided to push on with further reforms, known as the Second New Deal.

This so-called Second New Deal succeeded in keeping the momentum of the New Deal going. In the Presidential Election of 1936, Roosevelt was re-elected with an increased majority. His opponent, Alfred Landon, won only two small states; Roosevelt won the other 46. Roosevelt won so convincingly because he had majority support from all except the rich businessmen. As far as most voters were concerned, however bad their life still was, they believed that Roosevelt was the best person to continue the recovery.

However, in 1937, when unemployment was still at a figure of 6 million, Roosevelt became concerned at the extent of government spending (and debt) and cut back on some programmes. The result was alarming; the country plunged back into depression. By the winter of 1937–38, there were over 10 million unemployed. The government had to respond by quickly increasing expenditure again. It was helped by private industries who had managed to invent and innovate during the decade.

The New Deal as a whole had provided the conditions for full economic recovery. Yet, in 1939, business was still 25 per cent less than it had been in early 1929 and unemployment was still nearly 10 million.

The New Deal had stalled by early 1939 – by which time the focus of attention was on events in Europe and Asia.

⊙⊙ links

See pages 132–133 for more details on the criticisms Roosevelt faced.

> **Did you know** ?????
>
> Invention and innovation: petroleum refiners were discovering how to get more high-quality petrol (gasoline in the USA) from crude oil, and how to use the residue for synthetic rubber and other products.

⊙⊙ links

For unemployment figures in the 1930s see the chart on page 122.

A *A cartoon commenting on the New Deal from a US newspaper, 1933*

The impact of the Second World War on American economic recovery

In 1939, war started in Europe and the majority of Americans wanted to stay neutral. Roosevelt realised that this was not an option and increased spending on defence. Congress eventually agreed to allow countries to purchase goods, including weapons, on a 'cash and carry' basis.

In 1940, most of Western Europe had been conquered by the Nazis and Churchill had become Prime Minister of Britain. Roosevelt gave Britain 50 old destroyers; in return, Britain allowed the USA to use some of its bases in North and Central America for its own protection.

In March 1941, Roosevelt got Congress to support the **Lend-Lease programme**. The USA supplied vast amounts of war material to Britain. America could no longer pretend to be neutral.

In December 1941, Japan bombed Pearl Harbour, the US air base in the Hawaiian Islands in the Pacific Ocean. The USA declared war on Japan. Hitler decided to support Japan by declaring war on the USA as well. Congress supported Roosevelt and formally declared war on Germany.

Between 1939 and 1941, the US economy began to recover from the 1937–38 Depression because of the stimulus of war materials being ordered. Unemployment was still high. However, from 1942 onwards, it fell to nearly zero, even though many women joined the labour force for the first time. When war started there were 1,600,000 men in the armed services. By 1945, there were 12 million. The Gross National Product (GNP) – that is, all the goods and services created in the nation – doubled between 1938 and 1944.

D Business activity in the USA, 1929–45

Expanding industries needed for war meant taking on the laid-off workers in the northern industrial areas, as well as encouraging the migration of 1.6 million people from the southern states. Some industries expanded enormously.

The Depression of the 1930s was a thing of the past. The New Deal's contribution towards the recovery is a matter of dispute among historians. At the very least, it changed the climate of opinion towards government intervention and paved the way for a much greater level of government control during the war.

AQA↗ Examination-style questions

6   Study **Source A** and then answer **both** questions that follow.
     In your answers, you should refer to the source by its letter.

Source A Unemployed labourers sign on for welfare benefit, 1936

(a) Using **Source A** and your own knowledge, describe the ways in which the
     New Deal tried to bring relief to those in need.   *(8 marks)*

(b) 'The Second World War was more successful than the New Deal in ending
     the Depression.'
     Do you agree? Explain your answer.   *(12 marks)*

7.1
To what extent did racial inequality exist in the USA in the 1950s?

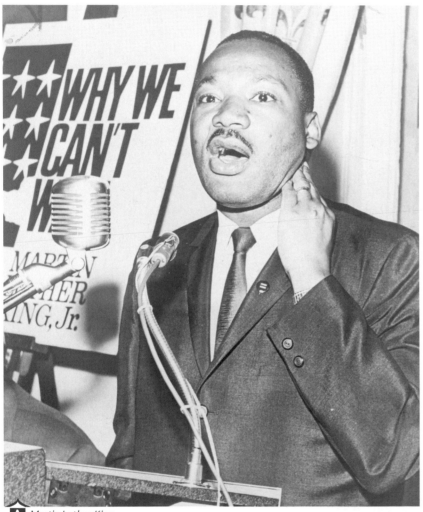

A *Martin Luther King*

Objectives

In this chapter you will learn about:

the extent to which racial inequality existed in the USA in the 1960s

how effective the methods used by members of the Civil Rights movement were between 1961 and 1968

how important Martin Luther King was in the fight for civil rights in the USA.

Timeline

Race relations in the USA, 1955–68

1955	The Ku Klux Klan continued attacks on Black Americans.
1956	Montgomery Bus Boycott.
1957	Racism at Little Rock Central High School.
1958	Battle of Hayes Pond.
1961	Freedom Rides.
1963	Freedom Marches and Washington March.
1964	Civil Rights Act.
1964	Martin Luther King was awarded the Nobel Peace Prize.
1965	Race riots began.
1966–67	Race riots continued.
1968	Martin Luther King was assassinated.
1968	Civil Rights Act.

This chapter concentrates on the issue of race relations in the USA from the 1950s onwards. It is important, however, to know that the issue started centuries earlier with the slave trade, which began in the 16th century and gathered pace in the 17th and 18th centuries. Even when slavery was ended in the USA in 1863, the formation of the Ku Klux Klan in 1866 and the Jim Crow laws meant that the fight for equality would be a long one. Segregation law made progress impossible, but actions by Black Americans and some White American supporters changed that, and the 1950s saw the start of a real push for equality for Black Americans.

Segregation law and attitudes in the southern states

The Jim Crow laws or segregation law were laws in the southern states of America between 1876 and 1965. They segregated whites from blacks in public schools, public places and on public transport. Alongside the Jim Crow laws, the 'Black Codes' limited civil rights and civil liberties of Black Americans. This included bringing in laws that made it impossible for Black Americans to vote, including a poll tax they could not afford to pay and a literacy test marked by a White American who would nearly always fail them.

Black Americans returning from the Second World War in Europe increasingly challenged this segregation. However, it was more difficult to challenge attitudes. Many businesses and white individuals created their own Jim Crow-type rules. This meant that many Black Americans found that they could not buy houses in certain areas, could not find work with certain companies and could not get taken on in certain types of skilled trades.

B *Black American drinking from a coloured-only water fountain*

C *Some of the Jim Crow laws*

State	Jim Crow laws
Arizona	The marriage between a white and a Negro shall be null and void.
Florida	The schools for white children and the schools for Negro children shall be conducted separately.
Georgia	All persons licensed to run a restaurant shall serve either white people exclusively or coloured people exclusively.
North Carolina	Books shall not be interchangeable between white and coloured schools.
Texas	Separate facilities are required for white and black citizens in state parks.

Task

1 How would the daily life of Black Americans be affected by the Jim Crow laws? How would this affect White Americans?

Ku Klux Klan

The Ku Klux Klan was founded in 1866 by soldiers from the Confederate Army in six southern states. Its purpose was to maintain slavery, gain revenge for the loss of the Civil War to the northern states and make sure that the Black Americans would not become equal citizens in the southern states at least! The Klan had been at its height before the First World War. In 1910 alone, 67 Black Americans had been lynched (hanged), but it was not until 1952 that the lynchings actually came to an end. Once the Civil Rights movement began its actions in the 1950s, Klan groups were re-established to challenge the movement. Houses were bombed, people intimidated and even assassinated. In Atlanta alone, over 40 homes were bombed in 1951–52. Many murders were never reported. As Black Americans could not vote and juries were often white only, blacks did not expect to get a verdict in their favour. Klansmen had close links with the local police and government, and used this to continue their intimidation.

Leaders of the Civil Rights movement were murdered, but at least some of the murderers were put on trial and found guilty.

D *Night-time rally of the Ku Klux Klan*

Task

2 a Read the section on the Ku Klux Klan. Do you think the Klan was still powerful in the 1950s?

   b How did Black Americans challenge the Klan in the 1950s?

Brown v. Topeka Board of Education

In 1896, the **US Supreme Court** decided that it was legal to have segregated schools as long as these schools were 'separate but equal'. In some cases they were, but in many areas the all-black schools were not as good. The daughter of Oliver Brown was expected to walk 21 blocks to her all-black school when there was a better, all-white school only seven blocks away. The **NAACP** (which was to be so active during the Montgomery Bus Boycott a few years later) decided to act. It asked a number of parents, including Oliver Brown, to try and register their children at the nearest school. All had been given places to go to at the nearest all-black school. They therefore decided, using the Brown family as their example, to take matters to the District Court.

The District Court ruled in favour of the schools using the old law 'separate but equal'. It agreed that Black American children might be better in mixed schools, but claimed that the schools were of equal quality and so did not need to do anything.

However, on 17 May 1954, the US Supreme Court ruled that segregation in schools should end.

Key terms

US Supreme Court: the highest court in the USA made up of nine judges, who decide on disputed points of law.

NAACP: National Association for the Advancement of Coloured People was formed before the First World War and fought for the rights of Black Americans in the 1940s, 1950s and 1960s.

High Court Bans Segregation in public schools

E *Headline from the* Chicago Defender *newspaper, May 1954*

> " *This decision was 'more important to our democracy than the atomic bomb'.* "

F *Extract from the* Chicago Defender *newspaper, May 1954*

Did you know ??????

In 1962, segregated schools still existed in Mississippi, South Carolina and Alabama.

In 1964, only two per cent of Black Americans in 11 southern states attended multiracial schools.

Once the decision was made, nothing happened. The judges of the US Supreme Court had not set a deadline by which to change the schools. President Eisenhower was worried because he believed that desegregation, if forced on people, would not work.

In the South it led to huge problems. In 1955, membership of the Ku Klux Klan rose dramatically. However, in March 1956, 22 southern senators issued the 'Southern Manifesto' in which they promised to do all that they could to end segregation.

In January 1956, all elementary schools in Topeka were organised by area rather than by colour of skin. This was seen as a victory for the Civil Rights movement.

Tasks

3 Explain what was meant by 'separate but equal'.

4 Who do you think read the *Chicago Defender*? Explain your answer.

5 Was the decision made by the US Supreme Court in 1954 a success? Explain your answer.

Rosa Parks and the Montgomery Bus Boycott

On 1 December 1955, Rosa Parks was arrested for breaking, not for the first time, the bus segregation law. She travelled on the same bus every night. On this occasion as the bus became full she was asked to move to another seat as her seat was now deemed to be in the white-only section of the bus. She refused and the driver stopped the bus and had her arrested for breaking the segregation law. Four days later, she was convicted and fined for her actions. She was immediately sacked from her job at the department store where she worked.

Rosa Parks was not the first Black American woman to be arrested for breaking the bus segregation law. However, in December 1955, Rosa went to members of the NAACP and agreed to become a test case, even though she knew it would lead to more trouble.

There was a one-day boycott of the buses, but this soon turned into a longer boycott, now known as the Montgomery Bus Boycott. Black Americans walked to work or started carpooling where available. Very soon the bus companies were losing money. White groups retaliated. Martin Luther King, who used his car to get people to work, was arrested and jailed for speeding in January 1956. Other carpool drivers and even people waiting for lifts were arrested. Martin Luther King's house was bombed, but the boycott continued.

For the next 12 months, over 17,000 Black Americans in Montgomery refused to use the bus service. Within a week, they had set up carpools that gave people lifts to work. At one time there were over 200 vehicles on the roads doing this, many of which were run by the local churches.

The boycott dragged on for nearly 12 months and, in the end, the US Supreme Court made bus segregation illegal. This new law began on 20 December 1956.

G *Official photograph showing the arrested Rosa Parks, 1 December 1955*

Did you know ??????

The bus segregation law stated that blacks could not sit at the front of the bus, regardless of whether the seats were empty or not. Blacks were only allowed to sit in the unreserved seating area at the back of the bus. If the bus was full, blacks would have to give up their seats to whites.

H *Black Americans in Montgomery walk to work*

In June 1956, two federal judges ruled that the segregation law was unconstitutional (against the law). The US Supreme Court agreed and, after a failed appeal attempt to change the decision, segregation was made illegal in the following month.

Segregation on buses was ended and the Civil Rights movement of the 1950s had its first major victory. Rosa Parks and her family, like Martin Luther King, became targets for racists and so she moved away from Montgomery to Detroit in 1957. She continued her work for the NAACP.

After the death of her husband in 1977, Rosa Parks founded an institute for self-development, which held summer schools called 'Pathways to Freedom'. In 1996, she was awarded the Presidential Medal of Freedom.

Task

6 a Explain why Rosa Parks was arrested.

b How do you think Rosa Parks felt after her arrest?

c How did the White Americans try to end the bus boycott?

d How does the bus boycott show that the Black Americans had not won the fight for racial equality?

Little Rock Central High School, 1957

In 1954, the US Supreme Court announced that segregation in schools was illegal. Arkansas, like many states in the south, did little to desegregate its schools. In 1957, a local newspaper, the *Arkansas State Press,* began a campaign to force desegregation. The school board and the city's mayor agreed that token efforts should be made to accept the law desegregating schools.

However, the Governor of Arkansas, Orval Faubus, did not agree. Nine black students had been registered to attend Little Rock Central High School, but when school started Faubus called out the **National Guard** in Arkansas to stop the black students attending the school.

On the first day, the nine black students expected did not turn up. On the second, they failed to get in when they were stopped by the National Guard. This was all seen on TV in the USA and many people were shocked. For the next 18 days they waited to see what would happen. For 18 days the President tried to persuade the State Governor, Orval Faubus, to obey the ruling, but he refused.

On Monday 23 September, the nine black students actually got into school. They were smuggled in by the delivery entrance. When a large white mob heard this, it attacked Black Americans on the streets, as well as the reporters from northern newspapers whom they assumed were sympathetic to the Black Americans. The police on duty did little. Many of them were on the side of the mob. In the end, President Eisenhower ordered 1,100 paratroopers of the First Airborne Division to 'escort' the Little Rock Nine, as they had become known, into school. The paratroopers stayed until November and the National Guardsmen, who were now under the direct control of the President, stayed for a year. Eight of the nine students also stayed for the year, but only one graduated due to the impossible conditions the students had to work in during their year at Little Rock Central High. Nevertheless, several of them went on to have very successful careers.

Did you know ??????

The first black students who attended Little Rock Central High School in 1957 became known as the 'Little Rock Nine'.

Key terms

National Guard: the reserve military force in the USA.

Did you know ??????

On 9 November 1999, the Little Rock Nine were awarded the Congressional Gold Medal by President Clinton.

In 2007, a commemorative silver dollar was produced to pay tribute to the strength, determination and courage displayed by the nine Black Americans.

The Little Rock Nine were invited to attend the inauguration of President-elect Barack Obama, the first Black American president.

1 The Little Rock Nine being escorted into Little Rock Central High School by the First Airborne Division

The events at Little Rock had a number of effects and not all were in favour of the Black Americans. Four parents of the students lost their jobs, membership of the Ku Klux Klan grew and the Governor became a hero in many people's eyes. Even though Little Rock reopened as a desegregated school in 1960, four years later only three per cent of its students were Black Americans. However, events at Little Rock did show the rest of the USA the scale of the problem.

Tasks

7 Design your own timeline for the events at Little Rock Central High School.

8 'The events at Little Rock Central High School meant that there were no winners and only losers.'

Do you agree? Explain your answer.

Did you know ??????

In August 1958, Governor Faubus and the school board closed Little Rock Central High School rather than continue with desegregation. Students had to attend high schools in other school districts. A year later, under pressure from court rulings, the school board was forced to reopen Little Rock as an integrated school.

Living standards of Black Americans

The Jim Crow laws played an important part in damaging the quality of life of most Black Americans. The laws limited the opportunities for work and many Black Americans moved north when they had the chance. This was called the Great Migration and it began before the First World War and continued up to, during and after the Second World War.

Black American sportsmen's chances to compete had been limited throughout the first half of the 20th century. (It was not until the late-1950s and 1960s that black sportsmen and women really began to participate in baseball and American football, as well as tennis and at the Olympic Games.)

The data in Source **J** is not typical for Black American lives. Unemployment was twice as high as for White Americans and 50 per cent of Black Americans lived in poverty. Yet the Second World War had shown many of them that life could be better. Standards of living had risen for all Americans during the war. White Americans took part in a consumer boom, buying washing machines, fridges and cars for their new homes being built in the suburbs.

However, although many Black Americans had fought against the racism of Hitler in the Second World War, change for the Black Americans was very slow. They were not allowed to live in the suburbs, but gathered in the towns setting up their own communities. These communities grew as Black Americans moved north to work in the new factories in places like Chicago. Those staying in the south continued working on farms, but also saw the growth in industries that were helped by the changes to race laws that were to follow in the 1960s. The difference was that Black Americans were no longer going to sit back and let things continue as they had done before the war, or after it – as events at Montgomery and Little Rock had proved.

J *Facts about the USA in the 1950s*

Population	151,684,000
Unemployed	3,288,000
Life expectancy (years)	Male 65.6 Female 71.1
Car sales	6,665,800
Average salary ($)	2,992
Labour force (male:female)	5:2
Cost of a loaf of bread ($)	0.14

K *Living in the inner cities in the 1950s and 1960s*

L *A new home in the suburbs in the 1950s and 1960s*

Tasks

9 Why did Black Americans leave the southern states in the first half of the 20th century?

10 a What can you learn from Sources **K** and **L**?

   b Which source presents the more accurate image of life in the USA in the 1950s? Explain your answer.

How effective were the methods used by members of the Civil Rights movement between 1961 and 1968?

The 1960s saw a large increase in the actions of those trying to establish racial equality. These actions were well covered by the press and TV and, as a result, the world watched events unfold in the USA. Freedom Rides and Freedom Marches showed the more peaceful approach, but as the decade progressed a new approach was adopted by some Black Americans. The Black Power movement was a direct challenge to the peaceful actions of Martin Luther King and his followers.

The Freedom Rides, 1961

In 1960, the US Supreme Court ruled that racial segregation on buses moving from one state to another (interstate buses) was illegal. This included ending segregation in bus terminals, waiting rooms and even restaurants. Two students tested the change in the law soon afterwards by daring to sit at the front of a bus. This led to the idea for the 'Freedom Rides'. A group of 13 people (seven black, six white) were picked to go on the journey from Washington DC through to the Deep South (where the most opposition would be).

They set off on 4 May 1961 on what was to be an epic journey.

> **Did you know ??????**
>
> During the Freedom Rides, the police commissioner of Birmingham, Alabama gave Klansmen 15 minutes to attack the Freedom Riders before sending in the police to maintain order.

Timeline

The Freedom Rides

4 May 1961	Freedom Riders left Washington DC.
14 May 1961	The Freedom Riders left Atlanta for Birmingham, Alabama. Members of the Ku Klux Klan got on to the bus and beat up some of the Freedom Riders and slashed the tyres.
15 May 1961	No bus driver was willing to take them further. Freedom Riders had to fly to New Orleans.
17 May 1961	10 riders arrived in Birmingham to continue the journey by bus. They were arrested and taken 150 miles away from Birmingham. They returned to Birmingham determined to continue, but could not find a driver.
20 May 1961	Riders were back on their way to Montgomery. Some Klan members attacked the bus. Some riders were seriously hurt.
21 May 1961	Martin Luther King spoke to the riders. The church he was in was surrounded and had to be protected by the National Guard.
24 May 1961	27 Freedom Riders travelled from Montgomery to Jackson. They were arrested for going into the white-only waiting room. 328 more riders were arrested by the end of the summer.

> **Did you know ??????**
>
> The Freedom Rides were organised by CORE – the Congress On Racial Equality.

A *'Getting on board the Freedom Rides', 1961. The Freedom Riders were given very good press coverage*

The Freedom Rides did, however, lead to the desegregation of the interstate buses. In September 1961, a regulation was passed to stop segregation on them. This came into effect on 1 November 1961.

Tasks

1 Do you think the Freedom Rides of 1961 were a success? Explain your answer.

2 Study Source **A**. How useful do you think it is to historians studying the Freedom Rides? Explain your answer.

■ Freedom Marches, the March on Washington, 1963

In 1962, Black Americans were facing unemployment and poverty on a larger scale than they had ever experienced. It led to the idea of marches for 'jobs and freedom'. In 1962 and 1963, there were hundreds of demonstrations and marches. In 1963 alone, there had been over 900 demonstrations in more than 100 cities with over 20,000 arrests. The most important was the march planned for August 1963, the March on Washington DC, the capital city of the USA and home to the White House.

The planning of the march was very carefully done, as protest organisers were worried that it might turn into a riot.

Worldwide Support ↙

Marchers set off from all over the USA. Where marchers could not get to Washington DC, there were symbolic marches to their own town halls, and abroad there were marches to US embassies.

The march was highly effective at bringing civil rights to the public's attention. The marchers met at the Washington Monument before dawn on 28 August 1963. At 11.30am, they marched to the Lincoln Memorial where Martin Luther King gave his famous 'I have a dream' speech.

Did you know ??????

The following were organised for the March on Washington DC, 1963:

- 292 outdoor toilets.
- 212 water fountains.
- 22 first-aid stations.
- 40 doctors.
- 80 nurses.
- 80,000 prepared lunch boxes.
- 5,600 policemen on duty.
- 4,000 troops.

Did you know ??????

The Lincoln Memorial was built in honour of Abraham Lincoln, who abolished slavery, and is located at the west end of West Potomac Park. Construction of the monument began in 1914 and was finished in 1922. For many people, the Lincoln Memorial is significant as it was on the steps at the front that Martin Luther King gave his 'I have a dream' speech.

C *Two black men standing by a Washington March sign*

D *Washington marchers heading towards the Washington Monument, August 1963*

In his famous speech, Martin Luther King spoke of his desire for a future where blacks and whites would live together in harmony as equals. King summed up the Civil Rights movement, highlighting the main problems and issues that still faced black people in the USA. He also stressed the importance of non-violent resistance, explaining that it was essential that though they faced injustice and violence, people must not react with violent protest. Lastly, King vividly expressed his vision of a better future for all people in the USA.

John Lewis was a poor black boy in Alabama, nearly the same age as Martin Luther King. In 2005, he wrote about how he heard Martin Luther King's message and felt compelled to devote his life to promoting the rights of black people. Later in his life, John Lewis became a Congressman representing Atlanta in the House of Representatives.

> " On the printed page it may be hard to see quite why this speech made such an impact; so much was in the manner of its delivery. But those of us who were there had no doubt. "

E *John Sergeant, political commentator, recalls his experience of hearing Martin Luther King give his famous 'I have a dream' speech*

> " *All of us knew that if we got involved in the civil rights movement, we could be beaten, or shot, or killed, but we faced the dogs and the fire hoses because we were longing to be free, and because Dr. King made us believe that it could happen.* "

F *John Lewis explaining the importance of Martin Luther King's 'I have a dream' speach*

In making his famous speech, Martin Luther King captured the feelings of the day and provided a vision of the future that Black and White Americans still look towards today. It is never far away from the thoughts of many Black Americans and, not surprisingly, was central to much that was said about the inauguration of the first Black American president, President Obama. Martin Luther King had a vision that at some point all men and women would be equal and people would not be judged by their colour, their personal history or their country's history. Having a black president in the White House in the USA appears to show that much of Martin Luther King's message has been achieved.

The US President, John F. Kennedy, decided to meet with the leaders of the Freedom Marches and congratulate them on their success. This was a major triumph for the organisers. The American nation now had to accept that the position of Black Americans was going to change and change for ever.

Sadly, less than three weeks later, four young girls were killed when a bomb exploded at the 16th Street Baptist Church in Birmingham, Alabama. This led to race riots in Birmingham, and by the end of the day, two more youths had been killed – a black 16-year-old was shot and killed by police after throwing stones at cars with white people inside and two white teenage boys riding on a bike shot a 13-year-old black boy, who was on a bike with his brother.

Martin Luther King spoke at the funeral for three of the girls, and more than 8,000 mourners, including three clergymen of all races, attended the service. No city officials attended.

The bomb in Birmingham was intended to stop the integration of schools and to scare Americans who had been demonstrating for an end to segregation. Instead, the bombing shocked the public and helped build support for civil rights legislation.

BIRMINGHAM

Activity

1   Use the internet to find out more about the 'I have a dream' speech.

Did you know ??????

The famous last section of the speech on the theme on 'I have a dream', was partly improvised and was not part of his prepared speech.

Did you know ??????

Two Klansmen were convicted in 2001 of the 16th Street Baptist Church bombing in Birmingham, Alabama.

In 1964, three civil rights workers were murdered. A Klan member was convicted of the murders in 2005.

In 1964, two black teenagers were murdered. James Ford Seale, a former policeman and deputy sheriff, was convicted in 2007.

Tasks

3   a   What led to the Freedom Marches?

   b   Why do you think the March on Washington was so carefully planned?

4   Do you agree with the interpretation in Source **B** that the 'I have a dream' speech is as important today as it was in 1963? Explain your answer.

5   Why was the meeting between John F. Kennedy and the organisers of the Freedom Marches so important?

6   Some historians might suggest that after the deaths in Birmingham, Alabama the March on Washington must have been a failure. Do you agree?

Following Martin Luther King's funeral, there were race riots in over 100 American cities including Atlanta, Nashville, Washington, Boston and New York. The rubbish collectors' strike in Memphis ended and an agreement was reached.

A further Civil Rights Act was passed a week later. Many believe it was passed as a result of King's assassination. The key points of this 1968 Act were as follows:

- You could no longer refuse to sell or rent a house to someone on the basis of race or colour.
- You could no longer advertise the sale or rental of a property and refer to race or colour.
- You could neither threaten nor intimidate someone living in a rented or bought house.

J Barack Obama becomes President of the United States. What would Martin Luther King have thought about a Black American in the White House?

Task

4 a Explain why Martin Luther King would have been very concerned about the race riots.

b Why do you think King's final speech is seen as important?

c How important was Martin Luther King in the fight for civil rights in the USA?

AQA Examination-style questions

7   Study **Source A** and then answer **both** questions that follow.
     In your answers, you should refer to the source by its letter.

Source A Troops outside Little Rock Central High School, Arkansas, September 1957

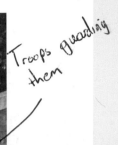

Different entrance? (We are else there)

Troops guarding them

(a) Using **Source A** and your own knowledge, describe events at Little Rock
     Central High School in 1957.   *(8 marks)*

(b) 'The Washington March of 1963 was the most important event in the
     American Civil Rights movement in the 1960s.'
     Do you agree? Explain your answer.   *(12 marks)*

8.1 How effective were the guerrilla tactics during the Vietnam War?

A American forces in Vietnam 1969

The war in Vietnam had begun during the Second World War. Before then, Vietnam had been part of the French Empire. During the Second World War, Japan took over the economy of Vietnam. A communist resistance movement, the *Vietminh*, was formed. After the defeat of Japan in 1945, the Vietminh, led by Ho Chi Minh, continued to fight against the French. In 1954, French rule collapsed after its army was defeated at Dien Bien Phu. The Geneva Conference of 1954 divided Vietnam into two countries along the 17th parallel. North Vietnam was communist, South Vietnam anti-communist. The USA began to support the South as the US government wished to stop the spread of Communism in Asia – the **Domino Theory**. Economic and military aid were provided, but the government of South Vietnam was not popular with its own people. By 1964, the USA was committed to protecting South Vietnam from the communist menace. This included the Vietminh threat from North Vietnam, as well as the many Communists in the south, known as the *Vietcong*, who were devoted to making South Vietnam communist.

Objectives

In this chapter you will learn about:

how effective the guerrilla tactics were during the Vietnam War

how the coverage of the Vietnam War in the USA led to demands for peace

why the US actions to end the Vietnam War were unsuccessful.

Key terms

Vietminh: a resistance movement formed by Ho Chi Minh in 1941 to fight against French and Japanese control. By 1945, it became communist and had taken control of North Vietnam.

Domino Theory: the American idea that, if Communism was not stopped in Vietnam, then other countries in South East Asia would fall 'like dominoes' into communist control.

Vietcong: the National Front for the Liberation of South Vietnam set up in 1960 to fight for Communism in South Vietnam. It was called the Vietcong by the Americans as a term of contempt. It was often abbreviated to VC.

B *Map of Vietnam, 1945–75*

Map labels: CHINA, NORTH VIETNAM, Dien Bien Phu, Hanoi, Haiphong, LAOS, Gulf of Tonkin, South China Sea, Hué, Danang, THAILAND, Dak To, Pleiku, CAMBODIA, R. Mekong, SOUTH VIETNAM, Bien Hoa, Saigon

1954 Geneva Conference partitions Vietnam along the 17th parallel

1968 My Lai Massacre

N

0   200 km

Timeline
Key events, 1954–75

1954	Collapse of French rule of Vietnam.
1954–64	US aid to South Vietnam government increased.
1964	Gulf of Tonkin incident.
1965	Operation Rolling Thunder.
1965–70	Use of chemical warfare by the USA.
1967	Vietnam Veterans Against the War formed.
1968 Jan	The Tet Offensive.
1968 Mar	Paris peace talks between the USA and North Vietnam. My Lai Massacre.
1968 Nov	Richard Nixon elected as President of the USA.
1969	Nixon ordered a gradual withdrawal of troops from Vietnam.
1970 Apr	US invasion of Cambodia.
1970 May	Kent State University protest.
1971	Vietnam Veterans' March to Washington. Fulbright hearings.
1972	North Vietnam invasion of South Vietnam failed.
1972 Dec	US bombing of North Vietnam.
1973	Paris peace talks – ceasefire and peace agreement reached.
1975 Apr	Fall of Saigon.

Tasks

1 Why did the USA become involved in Vietnam?

2 Look at the map in Source **B**. What difficulties do you think the US Government might have in protecting South Vietnam from North Vietnam?

The theory of guerrilla warfare

The basic aim of guerrilla warfare is to avoid a pitched battle with the enemy. The Vietcong used this as they could never hope to defeat the might of US forces in a battle. Their aim was to attack US troops in small groups, and then disappear into the surrounding countryside. The success of guerrilla warfare depended upon the support of the local people; to hide the Vietcong, as well as provide food and shelter. Eventually, the guerrillas would hope to wear down the Americans and destroy their morale in fighting an enemy that they could not see. This would then allow the Vietcong to take control of the areas where the Americans were stronger – the towns and cities of South Vietnam.

Guerrilla tactics

The Vietcong were recruited mainly from men and women who lived in South Vietnam. Other recruits came from North Vietnam. The Vietcong lived and worked within the village communities and became part of the village. By following the Code of Conduct, they could win the support of the local people. This support from the villagers was the key to the guerrilla tactics used by the Vietcong – without it they would have had no place to hide. The Vietcong also tried to persuade villagers to join them in the struggle so they often targeted officials of the South Vietnam government who would be unpopular with the villagers – the tax collector or the police – and kidnapped and murdered them.

The Vietcong also managed to get into camps of the US soldiers doing simple tasks like washing and cleaning. As one army officer bitterly said:

'What's a civilian? Somebody who works for us in the day and puts on VC pyjamas at night.'

However, the Vietcong were also soldiers, trained to fight in the tactics of guerrilla warfare. Direct face-to-face combat with the American or South Vietnamese armies was avoided instead they preferred tactics that were small scale. They would ambush an American or South Vietnamese patrol, and kill or capture the men in the unit – if captured, the enemy was tortured before being killed. They would set booby traps or plant bombs on known routes of enemy patrols. Having done their work, the Vietcong would then disappear into the countryside and the safety of their villages. These 'hit and run' tactics made it difficult for the Americans to know the enemy, let alone defeat them.

> 66 *You never knew who was the enemy and who was the friend. They all looked alike. They all dressed alike. They were all Vietnamese. Some of them were Vietcong.* 99
>
> Taken from Karnow, S. (1983) Vietnam: A History

D *Observations by a soldier who served in Vietnam*

An important aim of the Vietcong was to remain safe from US attack. They could not always assume that they would be safe in the villages or safe from American bombing. So they built networks of tunnels below ground in the countryside in which to live and hide. These tunnels catered for the needs of the Vietcong – they included weapon stores, sleeping quarters, kitchens and hospitals. They were strongly protected. As well as being difficult to find, they were booby trapped and trip wired at the entrances and throughout the tunnel. US propaganda claimed that the tunnels were built because the American bombing tactics were working. In fact, the opposite was true – the tunnel systems showed the level of organisation and determination of the Vietcong.

> 66
> 1 Be polite.
> 2 Be fair.
> 3 Return anything borrowed.
> 4 Do not damage crops.
> 5 Do not flirt with women. 99

C *Extract from the Vietminh Code of Conduct*

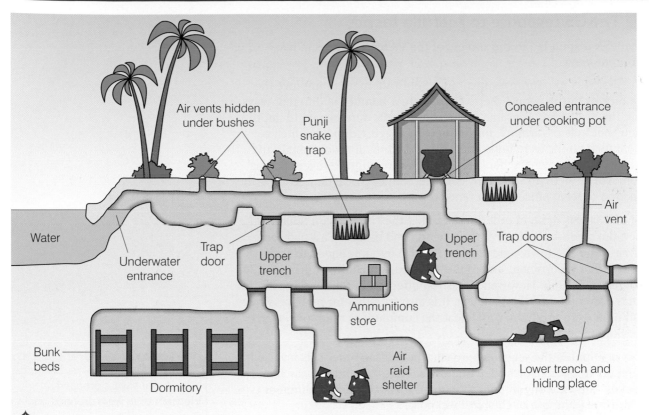

E *Diagram of a Vietcong tunnel network*

The Vietcong needed to be supplied with equipment and weapons. These supplies could only come from North Vietnam. Thousands of routes were developed all across the countryside linking North Vietnam to the South. The supply routes were often bombed by American planes and the supplies were destroyed. This could have a damaging effect on the North Vietnamese war effort.

To try to avoid this, the Communists developed supply routes from North Vietnam through the neighbouring countries of Laos and Cambodia and then into South Vietnam. This was called the Ho Chi Minh Trail. It was over 600 miles in length and in some places more than 50 miles wide. It had bridges to cross streams and embankments to cut through hills. Thousands of people worked around the clock to keep the Trail open. There were also 'dummy' routes leading from it to confuse the aerial photography of the Americans. The dense tropical forest through which it passed also provided good cover. Even so, the Ho Chi Minh Trail was often bombed by American warplanes. Despite all the difficulties of enemy bombing, monsoon rains and the constant damp of the rainforest, the supply routes were never closed. This allowed the Vietcong to continue with their constant attacks on the US troops.

> **Did you know** ??????
>
> The Ho Chi Minh Trail was a complex maze of truck routes, foot and bicycle paths, and river transportation systems. According to the US National Security Agency's official history of the war, the Trail system was 'one of the great achievements of military engineering of the 20th century'.

Task

3 Look at the evidence in this section on guerrilla tactics. List five points that help to explain why the tactics used by the Vietcong were successful.

The US response to guerrilla tactics

The USA responded to the success of the Vietcong tactics in two different ways.

The first was to pour investment into South Vietnam to improve the conditions of the people there. There were a number of different ways that this was done. Peasants in the countryside were helped to improve their methods of farming, for example by digging drainage ditches. Communications were improved by the building of roads, canals and bridges. In the towns, schools and clinics were built. Refugees fleeing from North Vietnam were provided with homes. Local democracy – the election of local officers – was encouraged.

All of this was done in order to show that the USA was on South Vietnam's side – to win over their 'hearts and minds'. This had some success and the towns and cities of South Vietnam tended to stay loyal to the government and to the Americans including during the Tet Offensive of 1968. However, it was less effective in the rural areas – the areas dominated by the Vietcong. It is also true that far more resources and men were used to try to defeat the communists than to win over the South Vietnamese.

This resulted in the second approach: the military one. This involved attempts to bomb North Vietnam into submission and to 'search and destroy' the Vietcong in South Vietnam. It also brought a different type of warfare – the use of chemical weapons.

In the early stages of the war, there had been incidents between the Communists and the Americans. In 1964, American newspapers reported that the US destroyer *Maddox* had been attacked in the Gulf of Tonkin by North Vietnamese patrol boats. It was a minor incident – no damage was done to the *Maddox* in an attack by three patrol boats. However, President Johnson exaggerated the incident in order to take action against North Vietnam. So with the approval of Congress, the USA responded with a bombing raid that destroyed patrol boat bases. It was a limited action and did not involve major bombing raids on North Vietnam. However, this showed President Johnson two things: that US military technology was far greater than that of North Vietnam; and that 'we have to meet aggression with action' as the USA must 'convince the leaders of North Vietnam that we will not be defeated'. The Gulf of Tonkin incident thus became an excuse for further US action. A second incident made US retaliation inevitable. In 1965, the Vietcong attacked a US base at Pleiku. Nine US 'advisers' were killed; almost 100 were wounded and 10 aircraft were destroyed. The USA reacted with **Operation Rolling Thunder**.

> **Did you know ??????**
>
> More bombs were dropped on Vietnam than were dropped on Germany and Japan in the whole of the Second World War.

> **Key terms**
>
> **Operation Rolling Thunder:** a concentrated bombing campaign on key strategic targets in North Vietnam, such as bridges, roads, railway lines and supply depots.

> **Task**
>
> 4 Which of the two American responses to the guerrilla tactics of the enemy do you think would be more effective:
>
> ■ to win over the people of South Vietnam
>
> ■ to defeat the North Vietnamese by bombing campaigns?
>
> Try to give reasons for your answer.

■ Operation Rolling Thunder

Operation Rolling Thunder did not bomb any of the major cities of North Vietnam. This was partly to avoid possible intervention by the USSR on the North Vietnamese side. However, the main reason was that the USA hoped that North Vietnam would back down once it had experienced the military power of the USA. In fact this did not happen, and the bombing campaign intensified. Instead of 'surgical' bombing aimed at particular targets, 'saturation' or 'blanket' bombing took place across North Vietnam including the cities. Huge B-52 bombers, each carrying 28 two-tonne bombs, battered communist territory. The bombing brought devastation to North Vietnam – but it did not force North Vietnam to surrender.

F A B-52 bomber

> 66 To increase the confidence of the brave people of South Vietnam, to convince the leaders of North Vietnam that we will not be defeated, and to reduce the flow of men and supplies from the North. 99

Taken from Kennedy, R. (1968) To Seek a Newer World

G President Johnson explains to the American people the reasons for the bombing of North Vietnam

> 66 The Americans thought that the more bombs they dropped, the quicker we would fall to our knees and surrender. But the bombs heightened rather than dampened our spirit. 99

Taken from Karnow, S. (1983) Vietnam: A History

H Comment by a North Vietnamese doctor on the US bombing, stated after the war

Task

5 Look at Sources **G** and **H**. Why are there differences in their interpretation of the US bombing campaign in North Vietnam?

The My Lai Massacre, 1968

> 66 *Inexcusable and terrible.* 99

> 66 *A sickening tragedy.* 99

K *Views expressed by President Nixon in 1969*

The events of My Lai

On 16 March 1968, nine US helicopter gunships carrying three platoons of soldiers landed near to the small village of My Lai on a search and destroy mission. About 700 people lived there. One platoon, led by Lt. William Calley, advanced into the village. Claiming that the village gave shelter to the Vietcong, Lt. Calley ordered that the village and those in it should be destroyed. No resistance was offered by the villagers. Eyewitness accounts reported that there seemed to be no males in the village apart from old men and boys. In the next two hours, around 500 unarmed men, women and children were killed.

> 66 *We started to move slowly through the village, shooting everything in sight, children, men, women and animals. Some was sickening. Their legs were shot off and they were still moving. They were just hanging there. I didn't fire a single round and didn't kill anyone. I couldn't.* 99

Taken from Bilton and Sim (1992) Four Hours in My Lai

L *From the diary of Thomas Partsch*

Just another incident?

It could be said that My Lai was just another incident in a violent war. Many Vietnamese civilians would suffer the same fate as the villagers of My Lai. It was just soldiers doing their duty. Lt. Calley seemed to suggest this when he said at his trial that the incident was 'no big deal'. It also summed up the problems the US forces had in fighting the Vietcong and in trying to defeat guerrilla warfare.

> 66 *Everyone who went into My Lai had in mind to kill. We had lost a lot of buddies and it was a VC stronghold. We considered them either VC or helping the VC.* 99

M *From the testimony of Varnado Simpson*

Did you know ??????

Three US servicemen who tried to stop the massacre and protect the wounded were criticised by US Congressmen and received hate mail and death threats. It was only 30 years after the event that they received recognition for their efforts.

Did you know ??????

Varnado Simpson and Thomas Partsch were American soldiers who participated in the My Lai Massacre. They both gave statements as part of the US Army's criminal investigation into the event. Partsch's diaries were also used as evidence. Simpson eventually committed suicide years later, unable to cope with the guilt.

Tasks

8 Read Sources **L** and **M**. Both are eyewitness accounts of My Lai.

a In what ways do they agree on what happened at My Lai?

b In what ways do the accounts of My Lai differ?

c Can you explain why there are differences?

■ Why is My Lai important in the Vietnam War?

The main reason why My Lai became important was that the American public learned of the killings. The news broke in 1969, 18 months after the event, when one of the US soldiers gave an account of the events on American TV. An investigation was held, statements from the troops involved were taken, and photos were released to the media.

American opinion was shocked. Some couldn't believe it or thought it was a Vietcong plot. Others were prepared to accept the killings and, to them, Lt. Calley was a hero. But the majority of Americans were horrified. It seemed that the inhuman behaviour of the US troops made them no better than the enemy – or the Nazis to whom they were compared. This was one of the key events that helped to turn the tide of American opinion against the war. Lt. Calley was the only soldier to face charges for My Lai. In 1970, he was sentenced to life imprisonment with hard labour. He was released in 1974.

N *Bodies of women and children killed at My Lai*

Tasks

9   Imagine you are an American citizen in 1969. What is your reaction to the My Lai Massacre? Give reasons for your answer.

10   Why do you think the My Lai Massacre happened?

How did the coverage of the Vietnam War in the USA lead to demands for peace?

TV and media coverage of the war

Vietnam has been called the 'first media war' and 'the first war fought on TV'. In previous wars, like the Second World War, the media had been censored and provided the information or 'spin' on the situation the government wanted. Vietnam was different: TV and other media reported on the war as they saw it. This coverage was not always favourable to the US forces; it was the media that had exposed the My Lai Massacre over a year after it had taken place. Furthermore, media coverage was constant. Every night, news bulletins and TV footage brought details of the war and the fighting.

> ❝ The war on colour TV screens in American living rooms has made Americans far more anti-war than anything else. The full brutality of the combat is there in close-up and in colour, and blood looks very red on the colour TV screen. ❞

A Statement by BBC newsman Sir Robin Day at a seminar for British armed forces in 1970

Newspapers and magazines gave full coverage of the war, including photographs. Two images in particular had a huge impact on the American public. One was the napalm attack shown in Source **J** (see page 167), the other showed the execution of a Vietcong suspect in the streets of Saigon during the Tet Offensive (Source **B** below).

The result of the media coverage was to turn the American public against the war. Much less was reported on the atrocities committed by the enemy. The North Vietnamese government kept a tight control on information. The image that came out of North Vietnam was of an undeveloped nation resisting the power of the USA.

B The Chief of Police in Saigon executes a Vietcong suspect, 1968

Task

1 Look at Sources **A** and **B** (on this page) and Sources **J** (on page 167), and **N** (on page 169).

a How reliable do you think the sources are in showing what the fighting in Vietnam was like?

b Should the American press have been censored in the Vietnam War?

■ Protest movements in the USA, 1968–73

Despite the impact of the media, many Americans continued to support the war. This was out of patriotic duty ('my country right or wrong') and also from a genuine fear of Communism. However, the media coverage did lead to a greater questioning of the war in some parts of American society. The draft (conscription) of young men into the armed forces added to the opposition, largely because many did not want to fight. It also came from resentment that richer, middle-class Americans seemed able to avoid the draft. These 'draft dodgers' went back to college, obtained medical disability certificates, or even left the USA.

This was the beginning of the anti-war Protest movement in the USA. It took a number of different forms. Many men tore up and burnt their draft papers in a public display of opposition. Anti-war slogans began to appear.

> 66 *Hey! Hey! LBJ!*
>
> *How many kids did you kill today?* 99

> 66 *Eighteen today, dead tomorrow.* 99

C *Anti-war slogans found in America*

Demonstrations and protest marches took place. In August 1968, 10,000 demonstrators went to Chicago to the Democratic Party Convention to protest against the war. Police used violence to disperse them. In November 1968, 35,000 people protested outside the White House. In 1967, the Vietnam Veterans Against the War had been formed. These were former US soldiers who had fought in Vietnam. In 1971, over 300,000 took part in the Vietnam Veterans' March. Many of the demonstrators had been severely injured; many wore medals received in the war. When they spoke out against the war, it had a deep effect on Americans.

Further protests were triggered by key events in the war such as the invasion of Cambodia in 1970 or the trial of Lt. Calley over the My Lai Massacre in 1970.

D *The Vietnam Veterans' March, 1971*

Task

2 **a** Which form of protest do you think would have had the biggest impact on Americans? Explain your answer.

  b Which form of protest do you think would have had the least impact on Americans? Explain your answer.

Reaction to the Tet Offensive

> 66 *Many observers believed that the (Communist) losses were so great that they would never again be able to mount an offensive on such a scale. The lack of civilian support for the North Vietnamese Army and the Vietcong strengthened the South Vietnamese government's claim that the war and the hearts of the people were both being won.* 99

Taken from Welsh, D. (1990) The Complete Military History of the Vietnam War

B *The impact of the Tet Offensive on the Communists*

> 66 *To American officials it all added up to a defeat for the Communists. But this was not the impression given by the reports and television footage of American newsmen. To them the Tet Offensive was an incredible shock, a great disaster, a clear defeat for the USA and South Vietnam.* 99

A statement by the Deputy Chief Historian for South East Asia, a state official. Taken from Sauvain, P. (1997) Vietnam

C *The impact of the Tet Offensive in the USA*

The US military saw the Tet Offensive as a victory. The North Vietnamese attack on Saigon and South Vietnam had failed and over 30,000 Vietcong had been killed. The Vietcong never recovered from these losses. From now on, the North Vietnamese army played the major part in the war – and it took it four years to recover. Even North Vietnamese officials accepted that it was a defeat. One said: 'We did not achieve our objective which was to stir up risings throughout the South.' Further proof of the North Vietnamese defeat seemed to be that North Vietnam now agreed to take part in peace talks.

However, the view of the American people was different. They watched the television footage, especially of the fighting in Saigon, and were shocked. It seemed as if the whole of Saigon had been destroyed. They read the press reports on the fighting and the results of it – thousands of civilian casualties, hundreds and thousands of refugees. How could this happen in an American strongpoint and in a war that the Americans were supposed to be winning? It seemed to the American public that this was a war that could not be won. It should be ended as soon as possible before many more American lives were lost in a hopeless war that could drag on for years. World opinion against the war and America's role served to reinforce this view.

This view was also shared by politicians. Congress refused the request of General Westmoreland, US Commander in Vietnam, for a further 200,000 troops to 'finish off the job'.

The Tet Offensive claimed one further casualty. President Lyndon B. Johnson decided not to seek re-election for the presidency in 1968. This left the way open for the Republican Richard Nixon to be elected as president. During his campaign, Nixon promised the American people that he would end the war. His Democrat opponent, Hubert Humphrey, only promised to reduce America's involvement in the war.

Task

1 **a** Who do you think gained most from the Tet Offensive: the Communists or the Americans? Explain your answer.

b Why did the American public believe that the Tet Offensive was a defeat for the USA?

■ US bombing campaigns and their impact, 1970–72

Peace talks between the USA and North Vietnam had opened in Paris in 1968 while Johnson had been President. North Vietnam had agreed to come provided the US bombings stopped. When Nixon replaced Johnson as president, he continued with the talks. They were to last off and on for five years – an indication of how difficult it was to find agreement between the bitter enemies.

In simple terms, the USA wanted South Vietnam to be independent and free from 'foreign' (i.e. communist) interference. North Vietnam wanted South Vietnam to be free from 'foreign' (i.e. American) influence. If this happened, North Vietnam felt that the whole of Vietnam could be reunited. It was also unclear what the position of South Vietnam was in any peace talks. Should South Vietnam be invited to attend? The USA demanded that it should be as it was an independant state. North Vietnam refused to recognise South Vietnam as an independant state and would not accept that it should be represented in Paris.

The USA had an additional problem – the growing opposition to the war from within the USA. This was a problem of being a democracy with a Government elected by and accountable to the people. The North Vietnam government did not have this pressure on them – as a Communist dictatorship, and therefore unelected, it could always show a united front towards the war.

Continued US pressure on North Vietnam

Despite the peace talks – or perhaps due to the slow progress – the USA continued to put military pressure on North Vietnam by continuing the war and the bombings. Nixon hoped that this would force North Vietnam to take the peace talks seriously. North Vietnam was still supplying the Vietcong with weapons along the Ho Chi Minh Trail through Cambodia and Laos. In 1970, Nixon ordered an invasion of Cambodia with the 'limited' objective of destroying the Trail. This extension of the war was unpopular in the USA. It was one reason for the Kent State University Protest. It also failed to close the supply route to the Vietcong.

Bombing raids in North Vietnam continued, aimed at keeping pressure on North Vietnam at a time when US troops were being withdrawn. By 1970, only 150,000 US troops remained from a previous total force of over half a million. Those who remained were less than enthusiastic about the war and morale was low.

∞ links

Look back to pages 172–173 to remind yourself about the Kent State University protest.

> 66 *1971 saw a series of stories revealing the massive heroin problem, the staggering desertion rate and the number of combat refusals among US troops. GIs were photographed carrying peace symbols or smoking pot from a gun barrel.* 99
>
> Taken from Knightly, P. (1975) The First Casualty

D *The low morale of US troops*

Paris Peace Conference and the US withdrawal, 1973–75

The peace agreement made at Paris had a number of important terms:

- US armed forces were to withdraw completely from Vietnam.
- US prisoners of war were to be released by North Vietnam.
- North Vie tnam recognised the government of South Vietnam, but the NVA could remain in areas of South Vietnam that they controlled at the time of the ceasefire.
- Elections would be held in the future to decide if Vietnam could again be united.

Le Duc Tho probably achieved more for North Vietnam than Henry Kissinger did for the USA. The Americans had left Vietnam. The ceasefire gave the NVA time to build up its strength and prepare itself for an attack on the South, and this would allow the North Vietnam government to take over South Vietnam at some time in the future.

For Kissinger, there was little alternative other than to pull the USA out of involvement in Vietnam. The war had become unwinnable and the political will to keep pouring troops into Vietnam had gone. For the people of Vietnam, the war was certainly not over. However, for many in the USA, there was only relief.

Did you know ??????

Henry Kissinger, the US Secretary of State, and Le Duc Tho, the chief negotiator for North Vietnam, were jointly awarded the Nobel Peace Prize for their work in bringing about the peace settlement.

66 *For the United States, the agreement signals the end of a nightmare. It promises the speedy and safe return of American troops and prisoners and an opportunity for fresh beginnings on neglected problems at home and abroad.* 99

Taken from The New York Times, *24 January 1973*

F *An American newspaper comments on the peace*

By April 1973, all US troops had left Vietnam. Only a small number of advisers remained. In return, North Vietnam released 600 prisoners of war – though the USA claimed that there were far more than this. In 1974, fighting between North and South Vietnam restarted. No US military help was given to South Vietnam. Congress passed laws to prevent the bombing by the USA of targets in Vietnam and Cambodia. The amount of financial support to Vietnam was also limited. North Vietnam was to take advantage of this almost complete US withdrawal.

Task

5 Who would you say gained more from the peace settlement: North Vietnam or the USA?

Give some reasons to support your decision.

■ The Fall of Saigon, 1975

North Vietnam continued the offensive into South Vietnam in 1975. As well as advancing from the north, it also attacked from Cambodia and Laos (even though this was against the 1973 agreement). This three-pronged attack divided South Vietnam and, more importantly, it split the ARVN forces.

Major cities fell to the Communists. Hue and Danang were taken with little resistance as South Vietnamese troops deserted in droves. Refugees from the north began to flee southwards towards Saigon and to what they thought was safety. This 'Convoy of Tears' further demoralised the South Vietnamese.

Saigon was not long in falling to the Communists. By the end of April 1975, they were in control of the capital. Many citizens of Saigon stayed to greet the conquerors. Others tried to escape as best they could – by road, moving further south; by air if they were lucky or rich; or by sea if they could squeeze into a boat and set off across the South China Sea.

As for the remaining US officials, they were airlifted by helicopter from the roof of the US embassy to awaiting warships. In this dramatic way the US presence in Vietnam came to an end.

G *Refugees fleeing from the communist armies*

H *The US airlift from Saigon*

Task

6   In 1968, the Tet Offensive showed that the USA and South Vietnam were still in a strong position to defeat the Communists.

Seven years later, Saigon had fallen to the Communists, the South Vietnamese government had collapsed and the last American had left Vietnam.

What do you think are the most important events to explain this change? Give reasons for your choices.

The Vietnam War – today

The Vietnam War caused much heart searching and much division in the USA. 57,000 US troops died in Vietnam; over 300,000 were wounded, many with permanent injuries. The scars left by the war still remain. Men who fought in Vietnam feel that they have not received the recognition they deserve for fighting for their country – unlike, for example, those who fought in the Second World War. At the same time, John McCain, the Republican candidate for the presidency in 2008, saw his years in Vietnam as a soldier and prisoner of war as a strong selling point in winning votes.

Vietnam, now ruled by the Communists, has had to rebuild. Almost 4 million Vietnamese died or were wounded in the war. Much of its terrain and resources were destroyed by bombing and chemical warfare. Yet, there are strong signs of recovery. One of the strongest ironies is that Vietnam now has a growing tourist industry much favoured by the West.

I John McCain, presidential candidate

Activity

1 Visit a local travel agent or use the internet (any major travel agent) to look for a travel brochure advertising a holiday in Vietnam.

Compare Vietnam today to what it was like in the period of war covered in this chapter.

What evidence is there in the advertisement that Vietnam has rebuilt itself?

If this is a group activity, try to make sure that different brochures are found by each member of the group.

AQA Examination-style questions

8   Study **Source A** and then answer **both** questions that follow.
     In your answers, you should refer to the source by its letter.

Source A A US soldier arresting a Vietcong suspect

(a) Using **Source A** and your own knowledge, describe the 'search and
     destroy' tactics used by the US forces in Vietnam.   (*8 marks*)

(b) 'TV and media coverage of the war was the main reason why the US
     withdrew from Vietnam.'
     Do you agree? Explain your answer.   (*12 marks*)

9.1 How far did political and economic inequalities lead to the Troubles in the 1960s and 1970s?

Objectives

In this chapter you will learn about:

how far the political and economic inequalities led to the Troubles in the 1960s and 1970s

why it was difficult to find a solution to the Troubles in the 1960s and 1970s

how far Ireland was from peace in the mid-1980s.

A *School children passing a constant reminder of the Troubles in Northern Ireland*

Timeline

Northern Ireland

1960s	Economy in Northern Ireland was in decline.
1965	Terence O'Neill began North–South Cooperation.
1967	University of Ulster was established.
1968	Start of civil rights marches.
1969	British army arrived in Northern Ireland.
1969–85	Terrorist campaigns of IRA and UVF were at their height.
1970	Internment began.
1972	Direct rule from London.
1972	Bloody Sunday.
1973	Power sharing.
1983	Harrods bombing.
1984	Brighton bombing.
1985	Anglo–Irish Agreement.
1986	Abolition of the Northern Ireland Assembly.

This chapter looks at the problems facing the people living in Northern Ireland between 1960 and 1986. It is important, however, to know that the issues in Northern Ireland have a very long history. This history is very important to the people who live there and, although you will not be examined on this, it is useful to have some idea of what those important historical events were. In 1916, an unsuccessful rebellion took place called the Easter Rising, soon to be followed by a civil war. In 1922, the Irish Free State was created in the south, independent but still part of the British Commonwealth. In the north, Ulster continued to be part of the UK and governed from Parliament in London.

In 1949, the Republic of Ireland was formed and the northern counties in Ulster stayed part of the UK. Northern Ireland had experienced an economic boom during the war, while the south had generally suffered an economic downturn. Once the war was over, however, the north began to suffer too and by the end of the 1950s the economy in Northern Ireland was in a poor state.

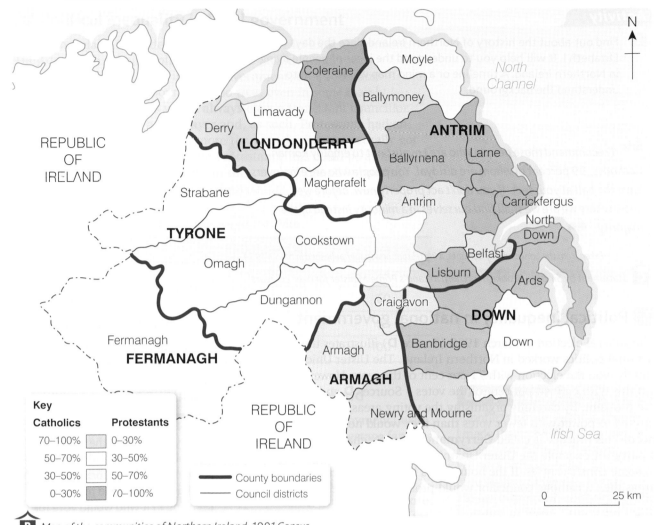

B *Map of the communities of Northern Ireland, 1991 Census*

Religious divisions in Northern Ireland

Religiously, Northern Ireland is a divided community. Protestants outnumber Catholics in Northern Ireland. About 38 per cent consider themselves Catholic, while 50 per cent consider themselves Protestant. What is important to remember is that, in some areas, Catholics outnumber Protestants. In Londonderry, known to Catholics simply as Derry, the Catholics are in the majority. Belfast is split between Catholic and Protestant communities and, as you will see, is at the centre of the problems in Northern Ireland. In other areas, the Protestants are the major religious group. Some Protestants choose to belong to the Orange Order – an organisation set up to defend the civil and religious liberties of Protestants. The order is organised into 'lodges', which can be set up where and when members wish. The Orange lodges are well known for their annual parades – often a flashpoint between Protestants and Catholics in the past.

The Orange Order is an organisation named after William of Orange, King of England, who defeated the Irish in a war in the 1690s. The group undertakes various activities, but its primary aim is to uphold the Protestant faith.

Did you know ??????

Ulster is another name for Northern Ireland. It is generally used by those who favour the union of Northern Ireland with Britain.

Task

1 Study Source **B**.

Draw up a table to show how Northern Ireland is divided by religion.

Terrorism and the Provisional IRA

The Provisional IRA was formed in December 1969 after the IRA convention voted to recognise the governments of Northern Ireland, the Republic of Ireland and the UK. Some members of the IRA were against it and they wanted to see a united Ireland with one government. On 11 January 1973, Sinn Féin had also split to create the Provisional Sinn Fein Party.

The Provisional IRA became steadily more violent in the 1970s until, in 1972, the official IRA declared a ceasefire. The **Provos** refused to do this and gained support amongst Catholics and Republicans.

The Provisionals were organised like an army, although its members were known as volunteers. These volunteers were members of a company, a battalion and then a brigade. There were five brigades in Northern Ireland, but the most important was probably the brigade in Belfast. In 1972, its membership grew rapidly after the events of Bloody Sunday.

In the Republic of Ireland, there was a Dublin Brigade and its job was to organise the importation of weapons to the north and to organise robberies to raise the funds to buy the weapons.

In 1977, the Provisional IRA **Green Book** laid out its tactics. It was quite simple. The IRA was to kill as many British troops as possible, bomb industries so that the economy suffered, make Ulster ungovernable and punish anyone who collaborated or informed on the IRA.

H *Provisional IRA members marching in Northern Ireland*

■ Terrorism and the UVF

The UVF was a Protestant Loyalist group formed in Northern Ireland in May 1966. It declared war on the IRA and, within a month, had killed a Roman Catholic barman. The UVF became much more active after the formation of the Provisional IRA in 1969. Its main method was the assassination of Catholics and as violence grew in the 1970s so did its attacks on Catholic communities. In December 1971, the UVF attacked McGuirk's bar killing 15 Catholic civilians. In 1976 and 1977, a small group of UVF members from the Shankill Road kidnapped, tortured and killed six Catholics.

The UVF was involved in bombings too and, on one occasion, UVF terrorists posed as members of the British army at a checkpoint on the border with the Republic of Ireland. Here, they killed members of the popular Miami Showband by planting a bomb onboard the band's bus. The band consisted of Catholics and Protestants. Two UVF members who happened to be part of the UDR were also killed when the bomb exploded prematurely.

I *UVF volunteers on the streets of Belfast*

∞ links

See page 189 for an explanation of the term 'UVF'.

> **Did you know** ??????
>
> The murder of a Catholic barman by the UVF in June 1966 led to the first leader of the group, Augustus 'Gusty' Spence, being arrested and sentenced to life imprisonment.

∞ links

See page 194 for an explanation of the term 'UDR'.

> **Did you know** ??????
>
> The UVF was responsible for the most deaths during the Troubles:
>
> ■ 350 civilians.
>
> ■ 8 politicians.
>
> ■ 41 other Loyalists, including 29 of its own members.
>
> ■ 6 members of the British army, RUC and prison officers.
>
> ■ 13 Republicans (mainly IRA).

Tasks

3 a Why did the Provisional IRA break away from the main IRA?

   b What methods did they use to try to get British troops out of Northern Ireland?

4 a What was the main aim of the UVF?

   b Describe the attack on the Miami Showband.

5 How did the Provisional IRA and the UVF make it difficult for a solution in Northern Ireland to be achieved?

This strike lasted until 3 October 1981 and, in the end, 10 Republican prisoners starved themselves to death, the most famous of these being Bobby Sands. He was the first man to go on hunger strike and, while in prison, was elected MP for Fermanagh and South Tyrone. Even the Pope's private secretary tried to persuade him to give up his strike, but he died six days later on 5 May 1981. On 7 May 1981, over 100,000 people attended Bobby Sands' funeral.

B *The funeral of Bobby Sands*

The death of Bobby Sands had a huge impact on events in Northern Ireland. Relations between the British government and the Irish government worsened. Support in the USA for the Republicans grew. A second death on 12 May led to further rioting. By September, the mood had changed. The families of the hunger strikers said that they would seek medical attention if their relatives in the Maze prison became unconscious. The six remaining strikers decided to call off their protest. Republican prisoners complained that the Catholic Church had put too much pressure on the families and forced them to end the protest. Changes in prison policy allowed civilian clothes, IRA prisoners to mix with each other, and increased family visits to prison. It was a propaganda victory for the IRA and the Republican movement.

Tasks

2   Why was there a hunger strike in 1980?

3   'There was little or no chance of a solution to the problems in Northern Ireland in 1981 after the death of Bobby Sands.'
    Do you agree? Explain your answer.

Mainland bombing

Mainland bombings were not new to the 1980s. The IRA's new campaign started in 1971 as the Troubles grew in Northern Ireland. In 1971, the Post Office Tower was bombed. Two years later, bombs exploded on the London Underground and a year later the Hilton Hotel was also bombed. In 1979, the Shadow Northern Ireland Secretary, Airey Neave, was killed outside the House of Commons. London was a clear target. In 1983, Harrods was hit and, in 1984, an attempt was made to kill the Prime Minister, Margaret Thatcher, along with leading members of the Conservative government.

C IRA bomb blast aftermath at Harrods in Knightsbridge, London

The Harrods bombing in London, 1983

A coded message from the IRA was received at 12.45pm. The police were searching the Knightsbridge area when the bomb exploded outside a rear entrance to Harrods. Three police officers examining the car containing the explosives were killed, as were three members of the public. Seventy-five people were injured by the explosion and the flying glass.

A second warning was given, claiming a bomb had been planted on Oxford Street. Police quickly evacuated the area. It was later found to be a hoax. The pre-Christmas bombing campaign was intended to frighten shoppers away from the capital.

A closer look

Did you know ??????

A memorial on the side of Harrods at Hans Crescent marks the spot where the three police officers were killed.

The Grand Hotel, Brighton, 1983

On 12 October 1984 at 2.54am, an IRA Semtex bomb exploded at the Grand Hotel, Brighton. It had been planted a month earlier by an IRA bomber and had been intended to kill the Prime Minister, Margaret Thatcher, and most of her Cabinet members. Five people were killed and over 30 injured as the bomb destroyed eight storeys of the hotel. The bathroom of the Prime Minister's suite of rooms was destroyed. She was in the next room working on some government papers. The conference opened as expected at 9.30am the following morning.

F Image showing the Brighton bombing at the Conservative Party Conference, including the extensive damage to the front of the building

66 *This attack has failed. All attempts to destroy democracy by terrorism will fail.* 99

D Prime Minister Margaret Thatcher, speaking on the morning after the bombing

66 *Today we were unlucky, but remember, we only have to be lucky once; you have to be lucky always. Give Ireland peace and there will be no war.* 99

E IRA spokesperson, speaking on the morning after the bombing

Activity

1 You can get a real feeling for the mainland bombing campaign by searching the internet. The BBC website 'On this day' can give you an insight into what it was like to live through these times. It also has extensive video footage of the news broadcasts of the day.

Working in a group, select one of the mainland bombings on the timeline on page 184. Use the BBC website and others to produce a five-minute news broadcast similar to those on TV. Present this to the rest of the class.

Task

4 **a** Why did the IRA follow a mainland bombing campaign?

b Which of these two bombings do you think had the bigger impact? Explain your answer.

- ■ Harrods bombing, 1983.
- ■ Brighton bombing, 1984.

The Anglo–Irish Agreement, 1985

Early in 1985, the British Secretary of State for Northern Ireland, Douglas Hurd, spoke of the possibility of new political arrangements to improve relationships between Northern Ireland and the Irish Republic. Talks soon began on this new political arrangement, despite the concerns of the Protestant Unionists. The Unionist leaders met with Margaret Thatcher in October 1985 to explain their reservations and, on 15 November 1985, the Anglo–Irish Agreement was signed.

The Anglo–Irish Agreement established an Inter-Governmental Conference, as well as the belief that any future changes required the support of the majority of people in Northern Ireland. It even established that a united Ireland would be created if the people in Northern Ireland wanted it. Unionists in Northern Ireland did not accept this.

Did you know ??????

Anglo-Irish Inter-Governmental Conference was made up of officials from the British and Irish governments. It had no powers to change laws, but could make proposals on certain issues. These included political, legal and security matters in Northern Ireland.

G *A Loyalist protest against the Anglo–Irish Agreement*

On 16 November, the Northern Ireland Assembly voted by 44 votes to 10 in favour of a **referendum** of all the people in Northern Ireland to either accept or reject the Anglo–Irish Agreement. The Assembly was sure the people would reject it. The Unionist MPs also announced that they would all resign within a month if the agreement was accepted, effectively bringing the Northern Ireland government to a halt. The Unionists did not want the agreement because they saw it as the start of a permanent union with Southern Ireland, while the Republicans did not think it had gone far enough. Their long-term aim was a united Ireland as one country, with one government, and the agreement did not reflect this.

Key terms

Referendum: a direct vote in which everyone is asked to either accept or reject a particular proposal.

◼ The abolition of the Northern Ireland Assembly, 1986

In November 1985, the Irish parliament voted in favour of the agreement by 88 votes to 75. This was followed two days later with a mass unionist protest when 100,000 people turned out at Belfast City Hall to oppose the agreement. This had little effect as the British parliament approved the agreement by 473 votes to 47 the following Wednesday. The Unionists then began their campaign to get rid of the Anglo–Irish Agreement.

Did you know ? ? ? ? ? ?

Ian Paisley addressed the crowd at the Belfast City Hall Rally. He argued that as long as the Irish Republic allowed IRA terrorists to take sanctuary there, it should not be allowed a say in the future of Northern Ireland.

H Loyalist protestors outside the Northern Ireland parliament building at Stormont during the strike that took place in March 1986

The election results in January showed increased support for the Unionists. In February, their leaders went to speak with Margaret Thatcher. Unconvinced, the unionist day of action followed in March. The strike was followed by riots, and shots were even fired at the RUC. The British government announced that more troops were to be sent to Northern Ireland. In May, Gerry Adams, the leader of Sinn Féin, also said he had doubts about the agreement.

By May, the Secretary of State for Northern Ireland decided to suspend the Northern Ireland Assembly and govern Northern Ireland from London. Unionist politicians refused to leave the Stormont building in protest, but it did not stop Northern Ireland from being governed from London. Protests and petitions followed as Unionists tried to end the agreement.

Task

5   How far from peace was Northern Ireland in March 1986?

■ Peace in Northern Ireland

It is difficult to know when the modern peace process began or when it started to have a real impact on the lives of Protestants and Catholics living in Northern Ireland. Some might say it started when the leader of the SDLP, John Hume, and the leader of Sinn Féin, Gerry Adams, met in 1988 for the first time and continued talks for the next five years. The IRA declared the end of military action in 1994, although a massive bomb attack at Canary Wharf in 1996 seemed to end any real feeling of peace.

I *Gerry Adams, leader of Sinn Féin*

Key profile

Gerry Adams

Adams was born in 1948 in West Belfast into a Catholic family. He was interned by the British in 1973, without trial, as he was suspected of being a member of the Provisional IRA, and not released until 1976. In 1983, he was elected President of Sinn Féin and, in 1987, he launched the Sinn Féin as a peace strategy. In 1993, he met with SDLP leader, John Hume, for the Irish Peace Initiative.

The Good Friday Agreement

Talks continued, however, and in April 1988 the Good Friday Agreement was signed. It gained support on both sides of the border in May 1988. Despite problems about the decommissioning of weapons, the Unionists agreed to join with Sinn Féin in government and, on 2 December 1999, powers were transferred back to the parliament building at Stormont. The issue regarding the decommissioning of weapons remained and Unionists and Republicans still found working together difficult, even after the IRA had officially got rid of its weapons in September 2005.

Devolution was finally restored to the Northern Ireland Assembly on Tuesday 8 May 2007, following the election of a four-party Executive of 12 ministers. The Rt. Hon. Peter Robinson MP MLA (Member of the Legislative Assembly) was elected as First Minister and Martin McGuinness MP MLA as Deputy First Minister. Peter Robinson was the leader of the Democratic Unionist Party. Martin McGuiness had joined the IRA in 1970 and was involved in the events of Bloody Sunday.

J *The Northern Ireland parliament building at Stormont*

AQA Examination-style questions

9   Study **Source A** and then answer **both** questions that follow.
     In your answers, you should refer to the source by its letter.

Source A A civil rights demonstration in the late-1960s

(a) Using **Source A** and your own knowledge, describe the civil rights marches of
     1968–69.   *(8 marks)*

(b) 'The hunger strikes of 1980–81 showed how far Northern Ireland was from
     reaching a peaceful settlement.'
     Do you agree? Explain your answer.   *(12 marks)*

10.1 How far did the years 1956–67 show how difficult it was to find a solution to the problems in the Middle East?

A *President Clinton and Yasser Arafat, Washington 1995. Finding peace in the Middle East has frequently involved the efforts of the US President*

Objectives

In this chapter you will learn about:

how far the years 1956–67 showed how difficult it was to find a solution to the problems in the Middle East

how close to victory the Arabs were in the 1970s

how close to peace the Middle East was by the end of the 1970s.

Timeline

The Middle East, 1948–79

1948 War of Independence (first Arab war).

1956 Suez Crisis.

1964 Foundation of the Palestine Liberation Organisation.

First Arab summit.

1967 The Six Day War.

1970 Start of hijackings.

1972 Munich Olympic Games.

1973 War of Yom Kippur.

1974 Oil War.

1975 Yasser Arafat spoke to the UN.

1977 Israeli Occupation of the West Bank and Gaza.

President Sadat of Egypt spoke to the Israel parliament.

1978 Israeli invasion of Lebanon.

Camp David Meeting.

1979 Signing of the peace treaty between Egypt and Israel.

Background to the problems in the Middle East, 1948–56

The background to this conflict dates as far back as the Romans when the Jews were driven from Palestine in AD 70 and AD 135. At the Basel Congress in 1897, the delegates there demanded a Jewish State in Palestine. At the same time, Arabs living in Palestine also believed that Arabs needed a homeland. The first Arab National Congress in 1913 made the same claims. By 1914, the two sides had become rivals.

Britain's commitment in Palestine

After the First World War, Britain was expected to look after Palestine. Promises of a homeland to both Arabs (the McMahon letter, 1915) and Jews (the Balfour Declaration, 1917) made Britain's position difficult. Increasing numbers of Jews began settling in Palestine and by 1947 Britain did not really know what to do next.

Britain had enough problems of its own recovering from the Second World War. Several events, combined with the constant threat of greater loss of life led to British public opinion demanding that the British leave Palestine. These included the killing of British soldiers in the bombing of the King David Hotel, the attacks on British soldiers as they ate in restaurants and the hanging of two British soldiers by Jewish terrorists for being 'spies'. Britain left in the years 1947–48 and the United Nations (UN) stepped in with its partition plan.

B *Map showing the UN Partition Plan*

The 'War of Independence' is sometimes seen as the first Arab–Jewish/Israeli war. The problems were to reoccur in the future. The Jews were outnumbered and fighting five Arab nations, yet they managed to turn defeat into victory. Their soldiers were more experienced and determined to win because they had everything to lose. As hundreds of thousands of Arab refugees fled to Lebanon, Iraq, Syria, Jordan and Egypt, the future freedom fighters for Palestine were given a reason to continue the fight, and the Arab nations of the Middle East a reason to refuse to accept the new nation of Israel in their midst. By 1956, the Arab–Israeli conflict was to raise its head again.

How close to peace was the Middle East by the end of the 1970s?

The Israeli occupation and the settlement of the West Bank and Gaza

In the second part of the 1970s, events in the Middle East were both strained and successful. On the one hand, Israel continued to cement its control over disputed territories like the West Bank and the Gaza Strip while invading Lebanon, yet, almost at the same time, continued to seek peace with Egypt through the **Camp David Agreements**.

The first Israeli settlements were established after the Six Day War. In this period, over 60 per cent of the land available was taken over by Jews who believed they had a right to settle in lands that they understood were theirs since biblical times.

Key terms

Camp David Agreements: two peace agreements signed by the Egyptian President, Anwar al-Sadat, and the Israeli Prime Minister, Menachem Begin, at Camp David on 17 September 1978. These were witnessed by the USA President, Jimmy Carter, and they ultimately led to the Israel–Egypt Peace Treaty in 1979.

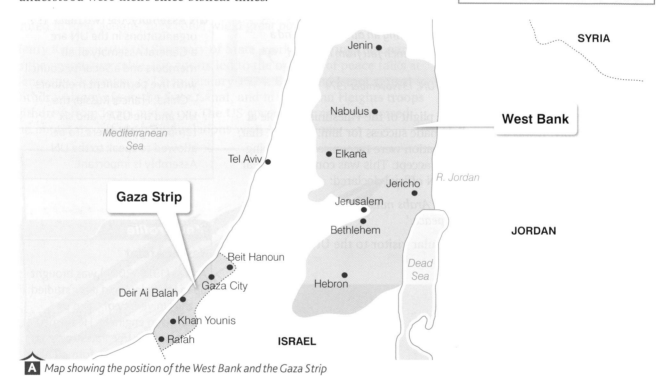

A Map showing the position of the West Bank and the Gaza Strip

The day after the 1977 elections, the new Israeli agricultural minister, Ariel Sharon, met with the leader of the settlers' movement to draw up maps of Judea and Samaria (the West Bank). They believed that the West Bank, Gaza and East Jerusalem were the biblical lands of the Jews and, therefore, planned to settle hundreds of thousands of Jewish citizens there.

To many outsiders, it appeared that the settlement programme was about surrounding Palestinian cities and villages; to make it impossible to withdraw Jews from the occupied territories of the West Bank and the Gaza Strip and so make Israel a larger and, therefore, safer country to live in.

Did you know ??????

The Camp David Agreements were the first peace deal between Israel and an Arab state.

Did you know ??????

Ariel Sharon later became Prime Minister of Israel from 2001 to 2006.

B *Two images of Israeli settlements in the West Bank. On the left, a simple building programme is underway. On the right, Israeli settlers are having to be protected as they lay claim to an old railway station as their new home*

" *The most important motive for settlement is historic. It was a mistake of mine too that for 30 years I did not stress enough the historic significance of establishing settlements in Judea and Samaria. This is indeed the birthplace of the Jewish people, and feeling your rights, which is a crucial component of security, depends first and foremost on the fact that you live in a place that's yours. To think that only the security factor is important was a mistake.* "

C *Ariel Sharon explains why the settlements of the West Bank and Gaza were important*

Did you know ??????

Judea is stated in the Bible as being the birthplace of Jewish people.

D *Number of Jewish settlements established in the West Bank*

Year	Number of Jewish settlements in West Bank
1967–70	20
1971–73	13
1974–76	11
1977	26
1978–80	74
1981–82	60

Tasks

1. What can you learn from the photographs in Source **B**?

2. Study Source **D**. Explain the growth of Jewish settlements in the 1960s and 1970s.

3. Using the information on these pages and Source **C**, what do you think are the main reasons why the Jews settled in the occupied territories?

President Sadat speaks to the Israeli parliament, November 1977

The new prime minister in Israel in 1977 was Menachem Begin. He was happy to make a deal with the Egyptians over the Sinai Desert, but was determined never to give away any of the perceived holy lands in the West Bank. In the USA, new president, Jimmy Carter, was also keen to find peace in the Middle East. This gave President Sadat of Egypt his opportunity; he shocked the world by announcing that he was willing to go to Jerusalem, to speak to the Israeli parliament and ask for peace. This angered the Syrian leader President Assad and the leader of the PLO, Yasser Arafat. The act of going to Israel showed that he accepted that Israel was a country in its own right and had the right to exist.

These discussions were a start. It was not, however, that simple. Sadat wanted the Jewish settlements in the Sinai to be destroyed, while Begin was prepared to pull out but not to destroy the new Israeli settlements. Further talks were needed and Jimmy Carter saw a role for the USA in these discussions.

E *The tension of this first meeting between Begin (on left) and Sadat (in middle) can be seen in this photograph*

Israeli invasion of Lebanon, March 1978

The first Israeli invasion of Lebanon

While Israel and Egypt were looking towards a peace treaty, the situation with other Arab nations was not as good. The PLO had moved to Lebanon in 1971. Linked with the growing power of the Syrians in Lebanon, the Israelis now saw this as the greatest threat to their nation. The Israelis saw part of the solution being their support for the South Lebanese Army (SLA), which was made up of Lebanese Christians. However, after an attack on an Israeli bus by the PLO that left 35 Israeli civilians dead, the Israelis invaded southern Lebanon. Palestinians and Lebanese were killed and, although the Israelis withdrew, they kept control of Lebanese lands on their border with Israel.

The Coastal Road Massacre, 1978

On the morning of 11 March 1978, a group of 12 PLO terrorists (*Fedayeen*) landed by boat from Lebanon just north of Tel Aviv. They killed an American photographer and then hijacked a bus full of bus drivers and their families on a day out. They headed north towards Tel Aviv and captured a second bus and moved the hostages on to it. They were eventually stopped at a police roadblock. The police were not trained to deal with such incidents and a long battle followed in which the PLO shot hostages who tried to escape. It may have been that more hostages were killed by the police than by the terrorists. The bus exploded and it is believed that 35 hostages died (including many women and 13 children). Seventy-one civilians were wounded. The Israeli security forces were criticised for the way they handled the incident and many Israelis wanted to know how the terrorists could land in Israel in broad daylight. This event triggered the Israeli decision to invade Lebanon three days later.

> **Did you know** ??????
>
> The leader of the PLO terrorists was a woman. Her name was Dalal Mughrabi. She had a school and summer camps named after her, even though she was involved in the killing of 13 children.

F *The bus destroyed in the Coast Road Massacre is now in a museum in Tel Aviv*

> **Task**
>
> **4** **a** Why would the Israelis be embarrassed by the terrorist attack known as the Coastal Road Massacre? Explain your answer.
>
> **b** Why would the leader of the terrorist group, Dalai Mughrabi, be seen as a heroine by the PLO and many Palestinian people, and have her name used in the way it was?

The second Israeli invasion of Lebanon

Lebanon continued to be a problem in the Middle East. The Israelis invaded Lebanon for a second time in June 1982, in the hope they could destroy the PLO. Over 19,000 PLO and Lebanese people, mainly civilians, were killed and the Israeli army lost 700 soldiers. The war dragged on for three years and, in the end, the PLO did withdraw to Tunisia, but Lebanon remained a difficult enemy for the Israelis.

> **Task**
>
> **5** Explain why the Israeli government might fear Lebanon.

The Camp David Agreements, September 1978

Timeline
Thirteen days of talking!

Day 1   Sadat of Egypt, Begin of Israel and Carter of the USA began almost personal negotiations.

Day 2   Sadat put forward his proposals. Carter suggested they sign there and then and save some time.

Day 4   Begin challenged Sadat's proposals line by line. Sadat and Begin fall out.

Day 5   The arguments continued. Carter raised the Palestinian homeland as an issue.

Day 6–10   The two sides were miles apart. Carter continued to refuse to allow the press in. Carter drew up new proposals.

Day 11   Sadat planned to leave Camp David.

Day 13   Discussions continued and, at last, the US President realised that an agreement had been reached.

The meeting was led by the US President, Jimmy Carter. It was held at his summer country home at Camp David. It was a very difficult time for all three leaders, but they eventually came to an agreement after 13 days of talking.

After the 13 days, the three leaders had produced two documents: 'The Framework for Peace in the Middle East' and 'The Framework for the Conclusion of a Peace Treaty between Egypt and Israel'.

Did you know ??????

Jimmy Carter received the Nobel Peace Prize in 2002 for his work 'to find peaceful solutions to international conflicts, to advance democracy and human rights, and to promote economic and social development'. He was the third US president to have that distinction.

Did you know ??????

Carter had to act as mediator between Sadat and Begin during the Camp David talks because they were very hostile to one another. The two avoided direct contact as much as possible during the talks, which meant that Carter had to have separate meetings with each of them and keep relaying their responses.

G *Jimmy Carter leading the Camp David talks*

The Framework for Peace in the Middle East

- Israeli military government would withdraw from the West Bank and Gaza.
- There would be a self-governing authority in the West Bank and Gaza.
- Egypt and Israel would not fight wars, but use the UN to resolve their problems.

The Framework for the Conclusion of a Peace Treaty between Egypt and Israel

- The agreement would be turned into a peace treaty within three months.
- Egypt would get back Sinai.
- All Israeli troops would be withdrawn.
- Israeli airfields left in Sinai could only be used for civilian purposes.
- Egypt will accept the existence of Israel and normal relations will follow.

> **Did you know** ??????
> Menachem Begin increased the number of settlements in the West Bank from 45 to over 100. He also made sure that any Palestinian opposition was severely dealt with. He continued his 'war' in Lebanon. He no longer had to fear Egypt.

The Washington Treaty, March 1979

In March 1979, the peace treaty was signed on the lawn of the White House. In the months following the agreements made at Camp David, it had become uncertain as to whether a treaty would actually be signed. Egypt was under huge pressure not to sign it from other Arab countries and the Israeli Prime Minister, Menachem Begin, did not want to consider an independent Palestine. Egypt was becoming isolated from other Arab nations. Nevertheless, the treaty was signed, and brought peace between Egypt and Israel for the first time.

> **Did you know** ??????
> President Sadat of Egypt became so unpopular that in 1981 he was assassinated by Egyptian soldiers at a military parade in Cairo. They felt he had betrayed all Arabs.

H *The signing of the peace treaty on the White House lawn*

AQA Examination-style questions

10   Study **Source A** and then answer **both** questions that follow.
In your answers, you should refer to the source by its letter.

Source A Egyptians crossing the Suez Canal at the start of the Yom Kippur War, 1973

(a) Using **Source A** and your own knowledge, describe the events of the
Yom Kippur War of 1973.

(8 marks)

(b) 'The signing of a peace treaty between Egypt and Israel in March 1979
showed that differences in the Middle East could be settled.'

Do you agree? Explain your answer.

(12 marks)

Glossary

A

Abdication: giving up all rights to the throne.

ARVN: the South Vietnamese army.

Atheism: the belief that there is no God.

Autocracy: rule by someone who has complete power.

B

Black Panther Party (BPP): a Black American organisation set up to promote Black Power and self-defence.

Blanket protest: prisoners refused to wear prison uniform and therefore wore their prison blankets instead.

Boom: a period of rapid economic growth with rising output, employment and profits – opposite of a slump.

C

Camp David Agreements: two peace agreements signed by the Egyptian President, Anwar al-Sadat, and the Israeli Prime Minister, Menachem Begin, at Camp David on 17 September 1978

Chemical warfare: the use of chemicals as a weapon.

Civil war: a war between political factions or regions within the same country.

Communism: refers to an economic and social system in which everyone works together for the common good.

Congress: the US representative assembly, the equivalent of the British parliament.

Constituent Assembly: people elected from the different parts of Russia to decide on the future way Russia should be governed. The elections had been ordered by the Provisional Government just before it was removed from power by the Bolsheviks.

Constitution: the way in which a society is governed with agreed rules.

D

Derry Citizens Defence Association (DCDA): an organisation sct up in 1969 in response to a perceived threat to the community of Derry in connection with the annual parade of the Apprentice Boys on 12 August.

Democrat: one of the two main political parties in the USA, the other being the Republicans.

Dictator: a person exercising absolute power, especially a ruler who has absolute, unrestricted control in a government without hereditary succession.

Dictatorship: a country, government, or the form of government in which absolute power is exercised by a dictator.

Domino theory: the American idea that, if Communism was not stopped in one country, then other countries in the area would fall 'like dominoes' into communist control.

Duma: a representative assembly, or parliament, first set up in 1905 in Russia as a concession by the Tsar.

F

Federal government: the US national government, based in Washington.

Fourteen Points: proposals by Woodrow Wilson, President of the USA, for a fair peace settlement that would aim to avoid future wars.

Freikorps **(Free Corps):** mostly unemployed ex-soldiers with extreme right-wing views and forming themselves into unofficial units in Germany.

G

Gerrymandering: the way in which local councils alter the boundaries of a constituency so that it always had more people living in it who would vote for their party rather than another.

Great Depression: the largest worldwide economic downturn that started in the USA in 1929.

Green Book: a training and induction manual issued by the IRA to new volunteers.

H

The House of Representatives and the Senate: the two Houses of the United States Congress.

I

Internment: the imprisonment or confinement of people, commonly in large groups without trial.

J

Jim Crow laws: a series of laws that were passed by the southern US states to discriminate against Black Americans.

K

Kaiser: the German translation of Emperor, e.g. Kaiser Wilhelm II of Germany.

Kristallnacht: (the Night of Brokcn Glass) Nazi coordinated attack on Jewish people and their property on 9 November 1938.

Kulak: a rich Russian peasant who was comparatively well off and often employed other peasants.

L

League of Nations: the international organisation set up after the First World War to solve disputes between countries.

Lend-Lease programme: arrangement between the USA and Britain during the Second World War allowing Britain to obtain materials from the USA without cash payment.

Left wing: those who believe that society should be more equal – at the extreme, Communists believing in total equality.

M

Mein Kampf: the book that Hitler wrote in prison in 1924 after the failure of the Munich Putsch. Translated, the title means 'My Struggle'.

N

NAACP: National Association for the Advancement of Coloured People fought for the rights of Black Americans.

National Guard: the reserve military force in the USA.

Nationalising: the act of taking an industry or assets into the public ownership of a national government.

New Economic Policy (NEP): started by Lenin in 1921, the NEP allowed peasants some control over their land and the sale of their crops.

NKVD: in Russia in 1934, the OGPU became the NKVD – the 'People's Commissariat of Internal Affairs'. It was the new name for the secret police, and the forerunner of the KGB.

Northern Ireland Civil Rights Association (NICRA): an organisation that campaigned for civil rights in Northern Ireland during the late-1960s and early 1970s.

NVA: the North Vietnamese army.

O

OAPEC: the Organisation of Arab Petroleum Exporting Countries.

OGPU: in Russia in 1922, the Cheka was reorganised as the OGPU – the 'Department of Political Police'.

Okhrana: secret police force of the Russian Empire.

Operation Rolling Thunder: a concentrated bombing campaign on key strategic targets in North Vietnam, such as bridges, roads, railway lines and supply depots.

P

Petrograd Soviet: a Russian workers' and soldiers' council.

Politburo: the voting group of Bolsheviks in Russia.

Prohibition: the period from 1920 to 1933 in the USA during which the manufacture, transportation and sale of alcohol for consumption were banned.

Provos: the Provisional IRA.

Pump priming: an expression used to suggest government spending would lead to economic growth.

Putsch: a rebellion; an attempt to seize power.

R

Referendum: a direct vote in which everyone is asked to either accept or reject a particular proposal.

Republic: a government with an elected leader rather than one that has a leader who inherits the title, such as a king or emperor.

Right wing: those who believe in a strong country with ordinary people having little power.

Royal Ulster Constabulary (RUC): the name of the police force in Northern Ireland between 1922 and 2001.

Russian Orthodox Church: the Christian Church in Russia.

S

Segregation: the policy of keeping different races apart.

Spartacists: Communists in Germany who took their name from Spartacus, a Roman gladiator who led a revolt in ancient Rome.

Special Powers Act: allowed the government of Northern Ireland to take any actions it felt necessary to maintain law and order.

SS: a group formed in 1925 as a personal guard unit for Nazi leader Adolf Hitler (an abbreviation of *Schutzstaffel*).

Student Nonviolent Coordinating Committee (SNCC): student organisation founded in 1960 dedicated to fighting segregation in the USA through non-violent and direct action.

T

Tsar: the Russian equivalent of Emperor.

U

Ulster Defence Association (UDA): a Loyalist paramilitary organisation.

Ulster Defence Regiment (UDR): an infantry regiment of the British army consisting of local volunteers intending to assist with security duties of Northern Ireland.

Ulster Volunteer Force (UVF): a Loyalist paramilitary group formed in 1966.

UN Assembly: the General Assembly of all members of the United Nations.

US Supreme Court: the highest court in the USA.

V

Vietcong: the American name for the National Front for the Liberation of South Vietnam.

Vietminh: a resistance movement formed by Ho Chi Minh in 1941 to fight against French and Japanese control.

Vietnamisation: the principle of ending the South Vietnamese dependence on the USA.

Index

A

abdication 34
Adams, Gerry 207
Agent Orange 166
alcohol, Prohibition of 67–70
Anglo-Irish Agreement *1985* 205–206
April Theses (Lenin) 17
Arab League 216
Arab Summits 215, 216
Arab-Israeli Wars 211, 212, 217–219, 223, 224
Arafat, Yasser 220, 225
ARVN (South Vietnamese army) 175, 178, 181
atheism 108
autocracy 6

B

Balfour Declaration *1917* 210, 211
banking crisis, US 126
Battle of the Bogside *1969* 191, 192
Bauhaus movement 46
Begin, Menachem 228, 230, 231
Black Americans
    Civil Rights Movement 144–151, 152–158
    in early 20th century 64–65, 66
    inequality in *1950s* 137–143
Black Panther Party 150
Black Power Movement 148, 150–151
blanket protests 201
Bloody Sunday *1972* 196
Bolsheviks 10
    and Civil War 24, 24–25, 26, 27, 28
    rise to power 17, 18–21, 22
    Stalin and 84
bombings, IRA campaign of 203–204

boom 118
    US *1930s* 54, 58–62
Britain
    and Palestine 210–211
    Suez Crisis *1956* 213, 214
    see also Northern Ireland
Brown v. Topeka Board of Education 139
Bruning, Heinrich 96

C

Calley, Lt. William 168, 169
Camp David Agreements *1978* 226, 230–231
Capone, Al 70
Carlos, John 148, 149
Carmichael, Stokely 150
Carter, Jimmy 228, 230
Catholics in Northern Ireland 185, 187, 187–188, 191, 195
censorship in Nazi Germany 106–108, 113
Cheka 22, 25, 82
chemical warfare 166
churches in Nazi Germany 101, 108
cinema 21, 62, 106
Civil Rights Acts 154, 158
civil rights marches, Northern Ireland 191
Civil Rights Movement, US
    Martin Luther King and 152–158
    methods used 144–151
Civil War 24
Russian *1918-21* 24–28, 29
Coast Road Massacre *1978* 229
collectivisation 88–89
communism 10, 29, 160
Communist Party 22, 82
    see also Bolsheviks
concentration camps 104
Congress, US 54
Connor, 'Bull' 153

Constituent Assembly, Russia 22
constitution 38
Coughlin, Father Charles 132
Craigavon, Northern Ireland 188–189
crime, USA *1920s* 70
culture
    Nazis and German 113
    USA *1920s* 61–62
    Weimar Germany 46, 47
Czech Legion 24

D

Dawes Plan *1924* 44
Dawson's Field hijacking *1970* 221
Democrats 54
Depression see Great Depression
Derry Citizens Defence Association (DCDA) 192
dictators 22
dictatorship 22
Domino Theory 160
Duma 6, 7, 15

E

Ebert, Friedrich 38, 47
Eden, Sir Anthony 213, 214
education in Nazi Germany 107
Egypt
    at war with Israel 217, 220, 223
    peace talks 228, 230–231
    Suez Crisis 213–214
Enabling Act *1933* 100

F

Falls Curfew *1970* 195
farmers and farming, US 121, 127
Fatah 220
Faubus, Orval 141, 142
Federal government, US 127
First World War
    Germany and 34, 35–37

Russia and 11–12, 23
USA and 54–55
Five Year Plans, USSR 90–92
'flappers' 71
Ford, Henry 58
Fordney-McCumber Tariff *1922* 57
Fourteen Points, Woodrow Wilson's 34, 35, 37
Freedom Marches *1963* 145–147
Freedom Rides *1961* 144–145
Freikorps **40**, 41
Fulbright Hearings *1971* 174

G

Germany 34
Depression and 95
and First World War 34, 35–37
Nazi Munich Putsch 49–50
Nazi Party 48–49, 52
Nazi rule in *1930s* 109–116
rise of Nazi dictatorship 95, 96–97, 98–108
Weimar Republic early problems 35–43
Weimar Republic origins 35
Weimar Republic under Stresemann 44–47
Gerrymandering 186
Gestapo 104
Goebbels, Josef 95, 98, 103
Good Friday Agreement *1988* 208
Great Depression 54
in Germany 95
in USA 73, 120–122, 123, 125
Great Terror, USSR 85
Green Book 198
Gropius, Walter 46
Grosz, George 46
guerrilla warfare 161–163
gypsies, Nazi persecution 116

H

Habash, Dr George 220
Harding, Warren 57
Hawley-Smoot Tariff *1930* 122

hijackings 220–221
Himmler, Heinrich 104
Hindenburg, General von 47, 96, 97, 104
Hitler, Adolf 48
Mein Kampf 51, 95
and Munich Putsch 49, 50
and Nazi Party 49, 52
rise to power 96, 97, 98–108
rule in *1930s* 109–110, 111, 114
Stalin and 85
Ho Chi Minh Trail 163, 177
Hoover, Herbert 72, 73, 122, 123
House of Representatives 123
Hume, John 200, 207
hunger strikes 201–202
hyperinflation, German 42–43

I

immigration, USA and 64
industrialisation, Russian 8, 90–92
internment 191
in Northern Ireland 195
Irish Republican Army (IRA) 189, 194, 198, 201, 202, 203–204, 208
isolationism, US 54–57, 64
Israel
Arab-Israeli Wars 211, 212, 217–219, 223, 224
invasion of Egypt *1956* 214
invasions of Lebanon 228–229
Munich Olympics *1972* 222
peace talks 228, 230–231
settlement of West Bank 226–227

J

Jews
Nazi persecution of 114–116
see also Israel
Jim Crow Laws 65, 137, 143
Johnson, Lyndon B. 154, 156, 164, 176

K

Kadets (Constitutional Democrats) 10, 24
Kahr, Gustav von 49, 50
Kaiser 34, 35
Kapp Putsch *1920* 41
Kellogg-Briand Pact *1928* 45
Kent State University Protest *1970* 172, 173
Kerensky, Alexander 16, 17, 20
Kerry, John 174
Khaled, Leila 221
Khrushchev, Nikita 83
King, Martin Luther 140, 145–147, 152–158
Kirov, Sergei 83
Kissinger, Henry 180, 223, 224
kolkhoz 88, 89
Kornilov, General 17, 19
Kristallnacht 1938 **114**–115
Ku Klux Klan 66, 138, 139
kulaks **29**, 84, 88, 88–89

L

Labour Front, German 109
League of Nations 37, 45, **56**, 57
Lebanon 228–229
left wing 38
in Weimar Republic 38, 39, 40
Lemass, Seán 188, 189
Lend-Lease Programme 134
Lenin, Vladimir 17
and rise of Bolsheviks 18, 20, 21
ruling Russia 22, 23, 29, 30, 31
death and funeral 77
testament 78
Lewis, John 146
Liebknecht, Karl 40
Little Rock Central High School, Arkansas 141–142
local government in Northern Ireland 187
Locarno Treaties *1925* 45
Long, Huey 132
Ludendorff, General 50

Luxemberg, Rosa 40
Lynch, Jack 190, 192

M

McGuiness, Martin 208
McMahon Letter *1915* 210, 211
Magnitogorsk, USSR 90, 91
Malcolm X 150, 151
Marx, Karl 10
mass production 58, 59
media, Vietnam War coverage 170, 171
Mein Kampf (Hitler) 51, **95**
Middle East
    background to problems 210–212
    changes in Arab tactics in *1970s* 220–225
    events *1956-67* 213–219
    seeking peace at end of *1970s* 226–231
Montgomery Bus Boycott 140, 153
Munich Putsch *1923* 49–50
My Lai Massacre *1968* 168, 169

N

NAACP (National Association for the Advancement of Coloured People) **139**, 140
napalm 166
Nasser, Gamal Abdel 213, 215, 217
National Guard 141
nationalisation 213
Nazi Party 50
    in *1920s* 48–49, 49, 52
    economic policies 109–110
    racial persecution 114–116
    rise to power 95, 96, 98–108
    social policies 110–113
New Deal, US 126–130, 131–134
New Economic Policy (NEP), Russian **30**, **76**, 88
Nicholas II 6–7, 11, 13, 15
NICRA (Northern Ireland Civil Rights Association) 190, 191, 196

Night of the Long Knives *1934* 102–103
Nixon, Edgar 152
Nixon, Richard 176, 177, 178
NKVD (Stalin's secret police) **82**, 84, 85
Nobel Peace Prize *1964* 154–155
Northern Ireland 184
    divisions and inequalities 185–188
    era of Terence O'Neill 188–190
    situation in mid-*1980s* 200–208
    Troubles in *1960s* and *1970s* 191–199
NVA (North Vietnamese army) **175**, 176, 178, 179, 180

O

OAPEC 224
October (film) 21
OGPU 82
    see also Cheka
oil wars *1973* 224
Okhrana 6, 7, 10
Olympic Games
    Berlin *1936* 105
    Mexico *1968* 148–149
    Munich *1972* 222
O'Neill, Terence 188, 189, 190, 191
Operation Rolling Thunder 164, 165
Orange Order 185

P

Paisley, Ian 188, 206
Palestine 210
    Arafat and 225
    Britain and 210–211
    Israeli settlement in 226–227
    terrorist groups 216, 220–222, 228–229
Palestine Liberation Organisation (PLO) 216, 225, 228–229
Papen, Franz von 97
Paris Peace Conference *1973* 180

Parks, Rosa 140, 141
peasants, Russian 8, 9, 16, 88, 88–89
Petrograd Soviet 15, **16**, 19, 20
Politburo 77
Popular Front for the Liberation of Palestine (PFLP) 220–221
Presidential elections 57
Prohibition **54**, 67–70
propaganda
    Nazi 95, 105, 113
    USSR 86–87
Protestant Unionist Party 188, 205–206, 206–207
Protestants in Northern Ireland 185, 187, 189, 194, 195
Provisional Government, Russia *1917* 16–17, 20
Provos (Provisional IRA) 194, 195, 198, 201
'pump priming' 129
purges in USSR 83–85
putsch 41
    Kapp Putsch *1920* 41
    Munich Putsch *1923* 49–50

R

race relations, US
    Civil Rights Movement 144–151, 152–158
    inequality in *1950s* 64–66, 136–143
racial persecution, Nazi policy of 114–116
Rasputin 13, 14
ratification 56
Recovery measures, US New Deal 128–130
Red Army 22, 25, 28, 29
Red Guards 17, 20, 22
Reds, *see* Bolsheviks
referendum 206
Reichstag Fire *1933* 98–99
Relief measures, US New Deal 127–128, 130
republic 34
    see also Weimar Republic

right wing 38
    in Weimar Republic 38, 39, 40,
        41, 49–50
Robinson, Peter 208
Röhm, Ernst 50, 102
Romanovs 13, 26
Roosevelt, Franklin D. 70, 124,
    125, 126, 131, 134
Royal Ulster Constabulary (RUC)
    191, 194
Ruhr, French invasion of 42
Russia
    in *1914–16* 6–10, 13–14
    1917 Provisional Government
        16–17
    1917 Revolution 15, 16
    Bolsheviks seize power 17–21,
        22
    Civil War *1918–21* 22, 24–28
    economic policies 29–30
    First World War and 11–12, 23
    see also USSR
Russian Orthodox Church 6

S

SA (Nazi army) 48, 49, 52, 95,
    99, 102
al-Sadat, Anwar 223, 228, 230,
    231
Saigon, Vietnam 175, 181
Sands, Bobby 201–202
SDLP 200
'search and destroy' tactic in
    Vietnam War 166
Second World War 134
segregation 64, 65–66, 137,
    139–143, 143, 144–145
Senate 123
Sharon, Ariel 226
Shostakovich, Dmitri 87
Show Trials, USSR *1930s* 84
Sinn Féin 198, 200
Six Day War *1967* 217–219
Smith, Tommie 148, 149
**SNCC (Student Nonviolent
    Coordinating Committee) 150,**
    153

Social Democrats 10
Social Revolutionaries 10
Solzhenitsyn, Alexander 86
Spartacists 40
special category prisoners 201
Special Powers Act 191
SS (Blackshirts) **52**, 102, 104
Stagg, Frank 201
Stakhanov, Alexei 92
Stalin, Joseph 77, 78
    comes to power 78, 80–81
    economic policies 88–92
    reinforcement of his dictatorship
        82–87
stock market, US 60–61, 72–73
'Strength Through Joy' movement
    111
Stresemann, Gustav 44, 45
Suez Crisis *1956* 213
Sunningdale Agreement *1973* 197
Supreme Court, US 65, 132, 133,
    139
Syria 216, 217, 223

T

tariff policies, US 57, 122
terrorism
    Middle East 216, 220–222,
        228–229
    Northern Ireland 198–199,
        203–204
Tet Offensive *1968* 175–176
Treaty of Brest-Litovsk *1918* 23
Treaty of Versailles *1919* 35,
    36–37, 56, 109
Trotsky, Leon 19, 23, 31, 77
    Bolshevik's rise to power 18, 20
    power struggle with Stalin 79,
        80–81
    and Red Army 25, 28
Tsar 6

U

Ulster Defence Association (UDA)
    195
Ulster Defence Regiment (UDR)
    194

Ulster Unionist Party 186,
    205–206, 206–207
Ulster Volunteer Force (UVF) 189,
    191, 195, 199
UN Assembly 225
unemployment in USA 120–121,
    122, 128, 131
US Supreme Court 65, 132, 133,
    139
USA
    the Depression 120–122, 123
    divided society in *1920s* 63–71
    international relations *1914–
        1920s* 54–57
    and Middle East 213, 214, 224,
        228
    New Deal 126–130, 131–133,
        134
    prosperity in *1920s* 58–62
    racial equality and Civil Rights
        Movement 144–151, 152–158
    racial inequality 64–65, 136–
        143
    Vietnam War 160, 164–169,
        170–174, 175–182
    Wall Street Crash *1929* 72–73,
        119
USSR 76
    1920s power struggle 78–82
    and Middle East 214, 220
    Stalin reinforces dictatorship
        82–87
    Stalin's economic policies 88–92
    see also Russia

V

van der Lubbe, Marcus 98
Vietcong 160, 161–163, 166,
    175, 176
Vietminh 160
Vietnam War 160, 182
    Fulbright Hearings *1971* 174
    guerrilla warfare and US
        responses 161–169
    media coverage 170
    Paris Peace conference and US
        withdrawal 180–181

peace talks and bombing
campaigns 177–178
protest movements in USA
171–174
Tet Offensive 175–176
Vietnamisation 178–180, 178

W

Wall Street Crash *1929* 72–73,
119
War Communism 29, 30
Washington Treaty *1979* 231
Weimar Republic, Germany 35
challenges to 40–41, 49–50
culture 46, 47
economy 42–43, 44, 46, 47, 95
and end of First World War
35–37
international relations 45
origins 35
politics 38–39, 46, 47, 96
Stresemann and 44
'Whites' 24, 25, 27, 28
Wilhelm II, Kaiser 34, 35
Wilson, Woodrow 54, 56
women
Nazi policies and 112–113
in USA in *1920s* 71

Y

Yom Kippur, War of *1973* 223
Young Plan *1929* 44
youth movements, Nazi 107–108
Yussopov, Prince 14

Acknowledgements

The authors and publisher are grateful to the following for permission to reproduce copyright material:

Text acknowledgements
p13 (Sources I and J) statistics as quoted in R. Radway *Russia and the USSR, 1900-1995,* Nelson Thornes; p13 (Source G) adapted from P. Ingram *Russia and the USSR, 1905-1991,* Cambridge University Press, 1997; p21 (Source G) Short extract from *Revolutions and Revolutionaries* by A J P Taylor, published by Athenium. Reprinted with permission of David Higham Associates Ltd; p22 (Source A) Short extract from a speech by Winston Churchill at Aldwych Club, April 11th, 1919. Copyright © Winston S. Churchill. Reproduced with permission of Curtis Brown Ltd, London on behalf of The Estate of Winston Churchill; p36 Short extract from *Peace Making 1919* by Harold Nicolson, 1933, Constable & Robinson. Reprinted with permission of Juliet Nicolson; p69 (Source E) Short extract from *The Long Thirst: Prohibition in America 1920-1933* by T. M. Coffey, Hamish Hamilton, 1975 edited; p89 (Source B) table from pg 39 *Russia and the USSR 1905-1991* by Philip Ingram, published by Cambridge University Press 1997. Reprinted with permission of Cambridge University Press; p91(Source G) short extract from *Behind the Urals: An American Worker in Russia's City of Steel* by John Scott, Boston: Houghton Mifflin, 1941; p99 (Source C) Short extract from *Aspects of the Third Reich* by H W Koch, Palgrave Macmillan, 1985. Reprinted with permission of Palgrave Macmillan, short extract from *Hitler: A Study in Tyranny* by Alan Bullock, Odhams, 1952; p107 (Source P) short extract from *The Naked Years: Growing Up in Nazi Germany* by Marianne Mackinnon, Chatto & Windus, 1987; p108 (Source Q) short extract from *Just Back from Germany* by J. A. Cole, published by Faber and Faber, 1938; p155 (Source E) Nobel Presentation Speech by Gunnar Jahn. Copyright © The Nobel Foundation 1964. Reprinted with permission; p172 (Source E) Quoted in *Time Magazine* 18 May 1970; p189 (Source I) Text extract from *The Lost City of Craigavon*. *The Lost City of Craigavon* was a DoubleBand Films production for BBC Northern Ireland www.doublebandfilms.com; p192 (A Closer Look) Extract *The Museum of Free Derry, a nationalist account of events in August 1969* taken from the museum website. Reprinted with permission.

Photo acknowledgements
Ann Ronan Picture Library 3.1A, 3.1D, 3.1G, 3.2B, 7.3D, 8.1A, 8.1F, 8.1N; **British Cartoon Archive, University of Kent** 5.2E, 5.2K, 8.3E, 10.2G; Corbis 6.1C, 8.3H, 9.2F, 9.3B, 9.3C, 9.X; **Edimedia Archive** 1.1D, 1.1H, 1.1I, 1.1J, 1.2B, 1.2C, 1.3D, 1.3H, 1.3M, 2.1A, 2.1L, 2.2C, 3.1J, 3.1L, 3.1M, 4.2C, 4.2E, 4.2F, 4.X, 5.1A, 7.1A, 7.2G, 7.3B, 7.3C, 7.X, 10.1H, 10.2D, 10.3E, 10.3H; **Germania Collection** 2.1E, 2.1H, 2.1M, 2.2A, 2.3A, 2.3E, 2.3F, 5.1B, 5.1D, 5.2A, 5.2L, 5.2N, 5.2O, 5.3B, 5.3G, 5.3K; **Getty Images** 1.3L, 3.1K, 3.2I, 3.2J, 5.X, 6.1H, 9.1G, 9.2C, 10.2I, 10.3Ba; **Istockphoto** 9.3J; **Courtesy of John Filo** 8.2F; **Photo12** 1.1Da, 1.2D, 1.3C, 1.X, 2.1J, 2.3C, 4.1D, 4.1E, 4.2A, 4.2D, 4.3C, 4.3E, 5.3H; **Press Association** 10.1C, 10.X; **Preußischer Kulturbesitz** 5.3I; **Public Domain** 1.1F, 2.3D, 3.X, 7.2H, 7.2I, 7.3J, 8.3I, 9.2D, 9.2E 9.3I, 10.3F; **Topfoto** 1.1K, 2.2B, 3.2H, 4.1A, 4.1B, 4.3F, 7.1K, 7.1L, 7.3I, 8.1J, 8.2B, 8.2D, 8.3G, 8.X, 9.1A, 9.1H, 9.1J, 9.2A, 9.2B, 9.2H, 9.2I, 9.3A, 9.3F, 9.3G, 9.3H, 10.1A, 10.1D, 10.1E, 10.1F, 10.1I, 10.1Ia, 10.2C, 10.2E, 10.2F, 10.3B, 10.3G; **United Archives** 5.2M; **World History Archive** 1.1A, 1.1B, 3.2A, 3.2D, 3.2F, 3.3C, 6.1A, 6.1B, 6.1D, 6.1F, 6.2A, 6.2D, 6.3A, 6.3C, 6.X, 7.1B, 7.1D, 7.1G, 7.1I, 7.2A, 7.2C, 7.2D.

The publisher would also like to thank the following who assisted with photographs which appear in this book: Ann Asquith and Jason Newman of Image Content Collections. Photo Research by Alexander Goldberg and Tara Roberts of Image Asset Management & uniquedimension.com